Hold the Blame
Hunt to Learn

Facilitating Serious Event Review Teams

By Mark Keough | 2025 Edition

A heartfelt thank you to my loving and patient wife, Patti, who offered her unlimited support to me during this project. What a wonderful person to journey life with!

Thank you to the Fire Department Safety Officers Association for their willingness to develop the Serious Event Review Team training. Special thanks to Eric Valliere (Assistant Chief Ret.), Past Chairman of the FDSOA Board of Directors, current Executive Director. Without his personal friendship and challenge to write this book (literally the day after I retired), I might never have written it.

If you ever write a book, I hope you will work with people like my editor, Mindy Blake, and publisher, David Serey. To describe them as kind and conscientious only begins to scratch the surface of their personal attributes and professionalism. Thank you.

Dedicated to the men and women of the fire service, especially the Mesa Fire and Medical Department, Mesa, Arizona, where I started and ended my fire service career. I will always fondly remember my part in such a remarkable family and humane mission. I am one of the lucky ones.

Preface

I never thought I had the capacity to write a book. In college I failed my first English 101 test. I had never failed a test before in my life! I was shocked. What dismayed me most was the reality that I had no idea WHY I had failed so miserably. My imagination took me to that space where I thought I should drop out of college and recoup some of my tuition money since I was a pay as you go type of student. No loans.

In desperation I went to my professor, Dr. Valentine, and I asked, "what did I do wrong? He was a fit man, blond short hair, blond beard and mustache, dark rimmed glasses, and rather pale skinned for living in Arizona. Dr. Valentine looked over my test for a minute then put it down on his desk and surmised, "You didn't learn English in high school, did you?" I felt defensive but the gods of wisdom told me to shut up and listen, so I replied, "No, I don't think so." A broad smile came across his face as he asked, "Do you want to?" I couldn't imagine being very good in college without a basic command of English, so I replied, "Yes."

Dr. Valentine confidently took me under his tutorship and made me buy another English book which started with topics like what's a noun, what's a verb and other basic grammar. Over the semester I learned basic English. Eventually we even tickled the topic of English theory – which was beyond anything I could have imagined.

Beyond learning how to write and understand literature, Dr. Valentine taught me a bigger lesson. He taught me mentoring relationships and learning can change life trajectories. Whether it be changing someone's life perspectives or someone's life purpose mentoring and learning changes people, organizations and culture if you mentor and teach others in earnest.

My desire to write this manual is an indirect way of mentoring fire service individuals, departments and hopefully culture toward the desire to learn from our failures and stop blaming individuals. Learning why we fail builds reliability and resilience, limiting catastrophic losses like people, major equipment, community confidence, and each other's trust. Dr. Valentine taught me learning after failure should be embraced because it improves performance in the long run. Failure is going to happen to us all. If managed well it should increase individual and organizational reliability and resilience.

For those who want to achieve more and are not sure what it will take I suggest you find a mentor. Experience has taught me the self-made man or woman is an illusion. Relationships are a necessary part of a better you and me. Perhaps you intuitively knew that truth, which is why you joined the team-oriented occupation of firefighting. We learn much more together. The method described in this book helps to keep us together under difficult circumstances.

Contents

Preface iv

Section One: Historical Influences 1

    Scapegoating – Early Influence 1

    The Industrial Age and Social Progress 3

    Heinrich – Dominoes, Triangles, and Icebergs – Models or Metaphors? 4

    Human Error – The Least Understood 8

    Emergency Response Decision-Making Research 10

    High Profile Organizational Failure 12

    Summation and Questions 16, 17

Section Two: Organizational Influences 19

    Culture 19

    Behavioral Based Safety Efforts 24

    Human Organizational Performance 26

    Complex Systems 32

    Reliability and Resilience 36

    Restorative Practice 38

    Bias 40

    Reduce Retributive Practices 44

    Accountability 46

    After an Adverse Event 46

    Summation and Questions 48, 50

Section Three: Review Considerations 53

    Getting Started 53

    Minor Events 53

    Assessing the Need for a Review 54

    When to Conduct a Review 56

    NFPA Prompts for Conducting Reviews 57

    Maintaining Confidentiality 59

    Making Complexity Transparent 59

    Surveying How Work is Done 61

    Is Root Cause Helpful? 62

    Summation and Questions 65, 66

Section Four: Discovery of Information Phase 67

    Collecting Equipment 67

    Collecting Witness Accounts 68

    Building Narratives 70

    Summation and Questions 71, 71

Section Five: Sensemaking and Analysis 73

    Some Common Factors to Consider 75

    Resilience Considerations 79

    Review Performance 80

    Summation and Questions 81, 81

Section Six: Sharing Findings 83

    Outcome Delivery 83

    Training Injury Example 83

    Narrative Story Versus Timeline Diagram 86

    Sharing Findings 87

    Summation and Questions 89, 89

Section Seven: Newer Perspectives on Safety 91

    People Help and Hinder (Obviously) 91

    Psychological Safety 93

    Success 93

    Falling on the Sword 94

    Black Lines, Blue Lines, (and Red) 96

    Seeking Zero 99

    Tracking and Reporting 100

    Summation and Questions 102, 103

Concluding Consideration 103

Closing 106

Section Question Answers 107

Section One | Historical Influences

"Trying to predict the future is like trying to drive down a country road at night with no lights while looking out the back window" – Peter Drucker

Understanding how historical influences shaped our current safety behaviors can help us shed unrealistic expectations within our safety programs.

My views on safety practices and culture evolved significantly as I explored broader safety approaches from other industries. Delving into the history of safety, I was surprised to discover that some prevailing safety values originated from flawed research and exaggerated claims, particularly from systems like root cause analysis. This revelation profoundly impacted my personal assumptions, values, and practices regarding safety.

My perspective on blame shifted dramatically. I once believed it was acceptable to identify and blame one or two individuals for an accident. It seemed logical, especially if a single person appeared to have made a mistake. My previous root cause thinking was to find the culprit, assign responsibility, and then move on.

In the fire service, our members often volunteer to admit fault and accept blame, and we allow them to be accountable so we can move forward. As my new understanding of learning (rather than blame) took hold, I began to reconsider the entire premise of finding a culprit just to return to business as usual. I realized that without genuine learning, we are destined to repeat similar mistakes. The individuals who made the original errors were often skilled professionals, in many cases better firefighters than I was. Simply telling everyone to "try harder next time" would not yield a lasting effect. Therefore, it became essential to first examine what influences our tendency to readily accept the easy solution of blame.

Scapegoating – Early Influence

Could scapegoating be inherently ingrained in our nature? As a faith community liturgical practice, it has a long and enduring history. In Old Testament biblical scripture, Leviticus 16 (circa 500 BC), the Israelite atonement ritual is meticulously described. While any ancient religious ceremony might seem irrelevant to modern life, its persistent adoption by communities, churches, governments, and corporations throughout history suggests its remarkable effectiveness. Read the scriptural verse that follows and visualize what took place.

> "5The community of Israel must give him (Aaron) two male goats and a ram. The goats are for a sin offering. The ram is for a burnt offering. 6He must cast lots for the two goats. One lot is for me. The other is for the goat that carries the people's sins away.... 9Aaron must

bring the goat chosen for me by lot. He must sacrifice it for a sin offering. ₁₀But the goat chosen by the other lot must remain alive. First, it must be brought to me to pay for the people's sins. Then, it must be sent into the desert as a goat that carries the people's sins away." [1]

As outlined in the first verse 5, the ram was designated for Aaron and his family. However, by verse 10, one of the goats is unfortunately taking on the sins of the people!

The practice was for the high priest to lay his hands on the second goat, publicly confessing the sins of the Israelite community. This act symbolized the transfer of the community's transgressions to the animal. This "scapegoat" was then led into the desert and released to fend for itself metaphorically carrying the community's sins into the wilderness, thereby removing them from the community. Tragically for the goat the desert was a harsh environment where its survival was unlikely.

This ritual was remarkably effective on social, psychological, and spiritual levels. The atonement ceremony offered comfort, restored a sense of order, and signaled a new beginning. It reinforced the community's belief in reconciliation with a just God. Imagine if it was possible, who wouldn't want to transfer all their misdeeds to a goat and simply walk away?

Blame in its modern form is the contemporary practice of scapegoating. We assign fault to others often without truly endeavoring to understand the multifaceted factors that contributed to a given situation. And, as it turns out, if any of us makes an error and is subjected to blame we are likely to endure various forms of "wilderness experiences" such as diminished credibility, profound remorse, marginalization, and in unfortunate cases, legal prosecution. Meanwhile, the rest of us can resume our daily lives with a comforting sense that the problem has been managed. We often utter phrases like, "They deserved that," or "I would have never done that," perhaps even, "He/she should have known better" or "He/she should have been more aware." In essence, modern-day blame is an echo of that ancient religious atonement ritual.

Scapegoating offers a seductive illusion that we can eliminate the bad apple(s) among us. Once blame has been apportioned, we are psychologically primed to revert to previous levels of complacent comfort while the systems we operate within remain fundamentally unchanged. It is convenient and it may even feel gratifying to declare that someone else is the problem. Psychologically, we all inherently desire to believe everything is under control.

I recall distinct feelings from my career when an individual was blamed for an adverse event. Often, I felt a sense of relief albeit accompanied by genuine sympathy for the person(s) involved. Safety investigations seemed simpler if one or two individuals bore the blame, especially if they accepted it voluntarily, as it appeared to be the expedient solution at the time. However, some of

---

[1] Leviticus 16:5-10, New International Reader's Version Bible, 2014,
https://www.biblegateway.com/passage/?search=Leviticus+16&version=NIRV on 10/2022.

those very individuals now express regret for not resisting and requesting a more thorough review of why their actions made sense to them in that moment.

I regret any harm I may have caused through my earlier, poor-quality safety investigations that failed to seek deeper context or a more complete understanding of why people made the decisions they did. Many contemporary investigative practices begin with the objective of determining what happened, who is responsible, and who will be held accountable. This type of pre-investigative intent unfortunately transforms investigations into sophisticated, modern-day renditions of the ancient atonement ritual. Whether someone misjudged a medication dosage, acted independently, or drove a tender at excessive speed, we dedicate substantial resources to naming, blaming and sometimes even shaming just to restore a perceived sense of order.

I see significant flaws when any investigator or organization initiates an investigation with the preconceived intent of discovering solely what happened, who is responsible, and who will be held accountable as stated above. This approach inherently sets the stage for something called confirmation bias. Confirmation bias can subtly influence any of us because our minds naturally gravitate towards data that supports any pre-investigative assumptions or needs that accompany our efforts. This again effectively becomes a veiled scapegoating process even if it is unintentional. We must diligently strive to understand how our personal and collective biases will inevitably interfere with the process of a balanced and fair review when we fail to manage them. More on this critical topic will be explored later.

The Industrial Age and Social Progress

Stepping back to the 17th, 18th, and 19th centuries industrial societies experienced an era of profound social shift towards collective responsibility. This new ethos demanded that commerce — from shipping and mining to railways — be held accountable for losses to citizens, insurers and governments. Social advocacy efforts effectively transitioned the focus of accident explanations from mere moral responsibility to legal obligations enforced by a burgeoning array of governing agencies.

In this era worker fatalities and illnesses often left surviving families destitute. Driven by societal moral outrage various agencies began to implement worker insurance schemes transferring the financial burden of harm back to employers. This pivotal development marked the budding stages of workers' compensation ideals, initiating the protection of worker well-being in the late 1800s and early 1900s.[2] For firefighters specifically, the formation of the International Association of Fire Fighters (1918) by the AFL-CIO was instrumental in developing work and wage protections.[3]

---

[2] *Foundations of Safety Science, A Century of Understanding Accidents and Disasters*, Sidney Dekker, Boca Raton, Florida, Taylor & Francis, CRC Press, 2019. Pg. 14-16

[3] *Fire Service Labor Management Relations: A Practitioner's Guide*, Bryan Jefferies, Phoenix AZ, pg. 18.

By the late 1800s, there was a growing demand for more scientific approaches to understanding work safety and investigating accident causation. Scientists were increasingly employed to prevent harm and meticulously analyze failures. This trend towards the systematic study of work has continued uninterrupted to the present day.

The rise of commercial transportation and the storage of large quantities of hazardous materials led to more severe accidents, fueling public outrage. Consequently, legislation was soon enacted granting wider powers to technical inspectors for accident prevention and empowering local government and regulatory agencies to investigate losses. This pattern of oversight and investigation remains a cornerstone of modern industry.

Today, the landscape of regulatory agencies, both private and public, has expanded and evolved significantly to meet ongoing demands for safer workplaces and thorough investigations. As a result, a firefighter fatality, for example, may now trigger investigations by the employing agency or corporation, an insurance agency, a law enforcement agency, an industry-specific body like the Chemical Safety Board, and state and/or federal safety agencies.

Herbert Heinrich – Dominoes, Triangles and Icebergs – Models or Metaphors?

In the evolving field of industrial safety Herbert Heinrich emerged as a pivotal figure whose influential theories shaped safety practices for decades. His seminal work introduced concepts such as the Domino Theory, the Accident Triangle (also known as the Heinrich Triangle), and the Iceberg Theory of costs (Figure 1). While initially presented as robust models for accident causation and prevention it's crucial to consider whether these frameworks function more accurately as metaphors or scientific models.

The Domino Theory suggests there is a chain of events that lead to an accident where the removal of any "domino" (like unsafe acts or conditions) can prevent the accident. The Accident Triangle models posit ratios of minor incidents to serious injuries and fatalities implying that addressing small incidents reduces the likelihood of larger ones. These concepts have provided some valuable perspectives for understanding and improving workplace safety, which have prompted a shift toward proactive prevention strategies.

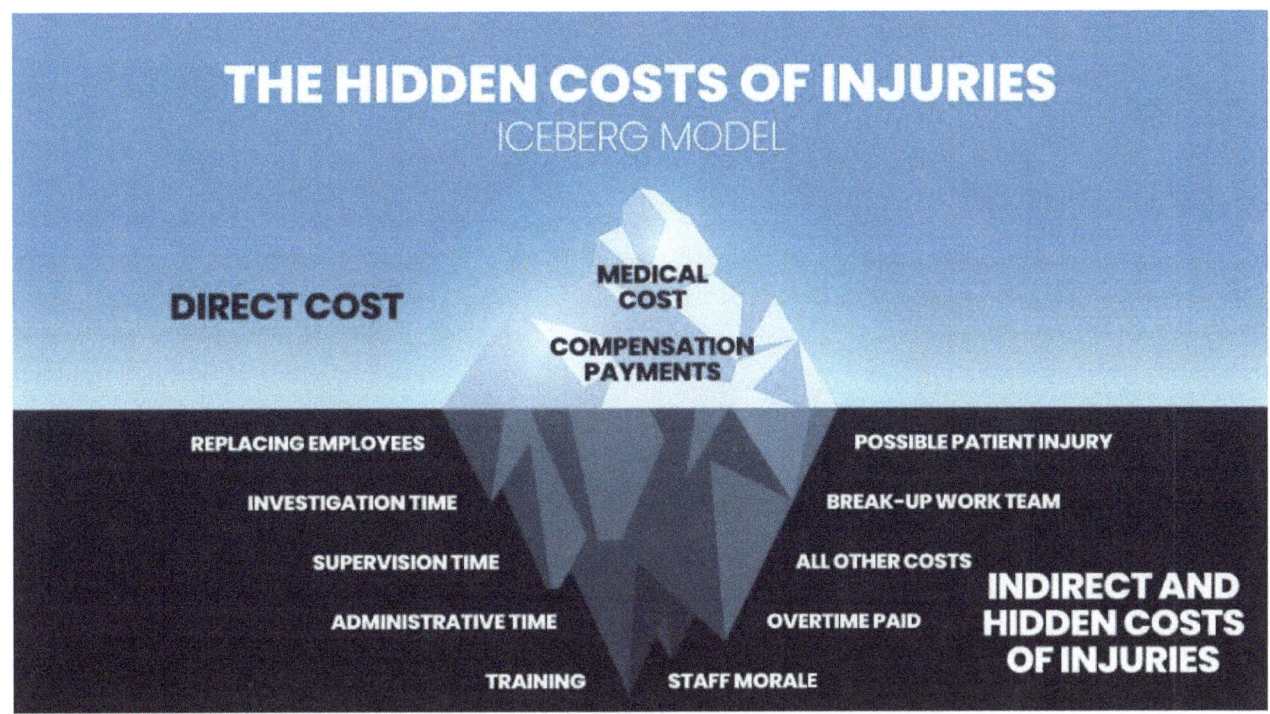

Figure 1. Heinrich's Iceberg Model of Costs

Herbert W. Heinrich (1886-1962), an employee of Travelers Insurance Company, published *Industrial Accident Prevention: A Scientific Approach*[4] based on extensive accident data he had access to through Travelers. His work introduced influential, yet problematic theories like accidents are linear chain reactions (like falling dominoes), accidents result from unsafe workers and that a direct relationship exists between minor and serious accidents (the accident pyramid). His work became widely accepted as truisms, yet his assumptions were less than scientific and were later refuted by Fred A. Manuele in *Heinrich Revisited: Truisms or Myths*.[5] Examining Heinrich's ideas is essential to understanding their limitations as many still regard them as factual.

Heinrich conceptualized accidents as linear chain reactions. He posited that unsafe worker actions combined with various surrounding hazards would initiate a sequence of events leading to accidents unless the chain could be broken. As Sidney Dekker explained in *Foundations of Safety Science: A Century of Understanding Accidents and Disasters*:

> "Heinrich used the metaphor of a row of dominoes to explain how distant causes led to injuries. According to his model, ancestry and the social environment give rise to character flaws in a worker, such as bad temper, ignorance, or carelessness. Character flaws give rise to unsafe conditions, mechanical hazards, and unsafe acts. These factors in turn lead to

---

[4] *Industrial Accident Prevention: A Safety Management* Approach 5th Edition, H. Heinrich, D. Petersen, N. Roos, McGraw-Hill Co., New York, 1980

[5] *Heinrich Revisited: Truisms or Myths,* F. Manuele, National Safety Council, Itasca, Illinois, 2002.

accidents, which lead to injuries and fatalities. Like a row of falling dominoes (Figure 2), the sequence could be interrupted by removing the right factor in the sequence."[6]

Figure 2. Domino Accident Theory

The domino metaphor suggests accidents are linear events where one factor inevitably follows another. However, when humans are involved, linear accident models fail to account for broader systemic, fiscal or organizational influences and the myriad human factors that affect performance. While linear causation models (like falling dominoes or Swiss cheese holes lining up) work well for simple tool or part breakdowns, they are inadequate for complex systems involving human operators with numerous internal and external influences.

Fire ground operations are a prime example of several complex systems interacting. During emergencies human operators perform autonomous tasks in unison with dynamic fire conditions under uncertain and certain circumstances continuously reinterpreting situations based on changing factors and differing vantage points.

Heinrich studied thousands of accident reports from various insurance and industry sources. He concluded that 88% of industrial accidents were caused by unsafe acts perpetrated by humans. However, the methodology behind this statistic is uncertain because the raw data was never published or found. Furthermore, much of the insurance claim information he used lacked a form field for explaining causation and was largely completed by supervisors who often exhibit a self-survival bias when reporting accident details. Meaning it wasn't due to supervision issues.

Heinrich also introduced the well-known accident triangle which likely illustrated a belief in the relationship between minor and major accidents. Following Heinrich, Frank Bird studied millions

---

[6] *Foundations of Safety Science, A Century of Understanding Accidents and Disasters*, Sidney Dekker, Boca Raton, Florida, Taylor & Francis, CRC Press, 2019, pg.88

of work hours across numerous industries to find support for Heinrich's pyramid model. Bird eventually developed different numbers (Figure 3).

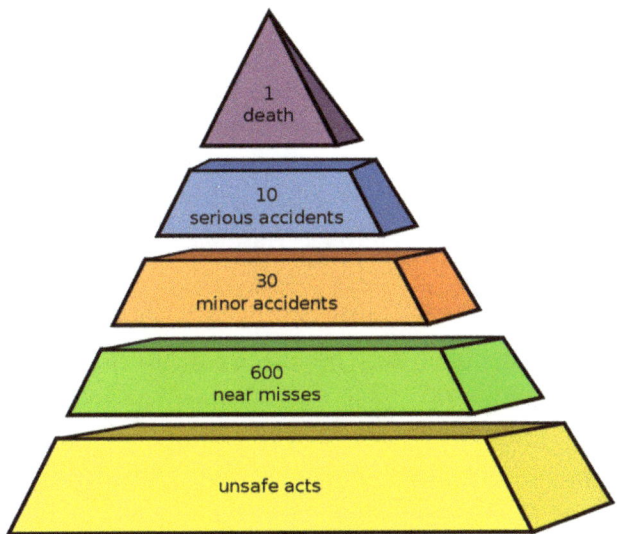

Figure 3. Bird's Accident Triangle Ratios

The Heinrich triangle ratio (300-29-1) and the Bird triangle ratio (600-30-10-1) led to the belief that eliminating minor accidents and injuries at the bottom of either model/metaphor would proportionally reduce more serious accidents. Dekker further explains,

> "The popular interpretation of Heinrich's and Bird's ideas follow the same logic; eliminate the small stuff, and the big safety problems (fatalities, containment losses, big crashes) will be reduced proportionally."[7]

Industry and safety practitioners believed, and some still do, that a relationship exists between minor and serious accidents. However, contemporary research does not support Heinrich's findings. Unfortunately, the legacy of these accident models (perhaps more accurately described as metaphors) for many has been a narrow focus on reportable accident and injury numbers as the primary indicator of organizational safety. Safety Officers (SOs) and Health and Safety Officers (HSOs) diligently collect these numbers and present them to leadership as a comparative measure against industry benchmarks or previous years. This practice is time-consuming and increasingly questioned in safety circles as largely meaningless since the data only gains meaning if we assign it (e.g., knee and ankle injuries have associated costs). The mere abundance or lack of injuries or accidents does not inherently predict the likelihood of a catastrophic loss or mean one agency is safer than another.

Instead, we need to identify descriptive metrics that help us build reliability and efficient operations thereby lowering the losses or damages incurred when failures occur. Do sprained

---

[7] *Foundations of Safety Science, A Century of Understanding Accidents and Disasters,* Sidney Dekker, Boca Raton, Florida, Taylor & Francis, CRC Press, 2019, pg.98

ankles truly describe unreliable or inefficient operations? Probably not. Does the lack of conducting post-incident reviews or critiques lead to less reliability or resilience? Yes, I think it does.

Heinrich's work also implied that some workers were inherently more accident-prone or less intelligent leading to a disproportionate number of accidents among a small percentage of the workforce. While the idea of simply selecting high-IQ or careful workers to improve safety is appealing research does not meaningfully support this belief. Because these assumptions were not adequately debunked for some time worker behavior (often labeled - human error) evolved into a default finding for accident causation.

Department Health and Safety Officers (HSOs) should drive the effort to ensure both reliability and resilience and be increasingly present in every aspect of fire department operations. While accident and injury statistics may play a role in confirming the effectiveness of controls, they are not the primary indicators of your organization's overall safety. In complex organizations like fire departments, understanding how relationships between intradepartmental divisions influences safety and efficiency is positive movement toward increased organizational safety. HSOs play a key role in making these relationships transparent.

Human Error – The Least Understood

Human error gained significant attention in human factors studies from the 1950s onward. The goal was to design error-resistant or error-tolerant systems by anticipating potential human errors and preventing them through work design. The Department of Defense heavily supported human factors research related to error as the advent of faster, higher-flying aircraft, advanced weaponry, and nuclear power demanded systems that could prevent human error given the non-survivable consequences of failure. While technological design advanced exponentially, the study of contributing human factors in technological operations struggled to keep pace.

By the 1970s, efforts to apply the best industrial investigative methods to accident analysis increasingly focused on humans interacting within complex systems. The Management Oversight and Risk Tree (MORT) was a notable initiative aimed at improving safety through system analysis, accident causation, human factors, error reduction, and measurement of safety performance (Johnson, 1973).[8] MORT significantly shifted safety considerations toward understanding systems and environments.

Although human error had been discussed since the early 1900s it became a primary subject of scientific study after the Three Mile Island nuclear accident in 1979. Human error was recognized as a critical problem requiring more attention in high-risk time-constrained industries. Two main schools of thought emerged from this research: Cognitive Psychology and Joint Cognitive Systems. These concepts, led by Dr. James Reason and Dr. Jens Rasmussen respectively, are straightforward.

Reason concluded that people make errors as a fact of everyday life. In his book, *Human Error*, he categorized human errors into four labels to describe accident causes:[9]

> Slips – attention failures
> Lapses – memory failures
> Mistakes – failures in understanding rules or lack of knowledge
> Violations – deliberate noncompliance with known rules

These labels are now widely used to explain human behavior due to their agreed-upon definitions and the substantiation of their presence through Reason's studies.

Rasmussen, along with researchers like Erik Hollnagel and David Woods, observed how humans managed increasing complexity in the workplace. Rasmussen and his team found that error was a reaction or a product of people and systems within a specific context of time and place. For example, a pilot in a cockpit or an engineer in a control room would act or react based on their limited understanding of how the systems were interacting at any given moment. His team concluded that human error was never the root cause of an accident. Rasmussen's research was pivotal for safety practitioners across industries, redefining human error as a symptom of larger or deeper system problems, much like a fever indicates an infection or systemic illness.

What does this mean for us? I think the research perspective we emphasize, whether individually or organizationally, can lead to different findings and consequently different short-term and long-term improvements. Reason's research focuses more on improving human behavior, aligning with Behavioral Based Safety (BBS) programs. BBS corrective actions will typically concentrate on motivation, training, policy changes, procedural adjustments, or other interventions designed to

---

[8] *The Management Oversight and Risk Tree,* W. Johnson, U.S. Atomic Energy Commission, Division of Operational Safety, 1973.

[9] *Human Error,* J. Reason, Cambridge University Press, Cambridge, England, 1990.

modify worker behaviors and reduce accidents. Rasmussen's research takes a broader view of the work system as it considers the context surrounding events that may appear to be human errors. In Rasmussen's framework investigators should examine work environments, the human-work interface, time constraints, goal conflicts, contextual understanding, and pressures present during the event. After comprehensive consideration and analysis, suggestions for system improvements can be made. I lean towards Rasmussen's work in this area, especially given that emergency services involve significant time constraints and firefighters often face competing goals or priorities.

Both perspectives offer valuable frameworks for investigations or reviews. I've found that when findings label an incident as a firefighter's slip, lapse, mistake, or violation, it becomes more challenging to foster openness and trust, potentially limiting organizational learning.

A strong caution: once "human error" becomes the definitive label, learning often ceases. Reviews that focus on broader system influences, worker contextual factors and human factors affecting decision-making are far more likely to enhance organizational learning.

Emergency Response Decision-Making Research

In the mid-to-late 1980s, Dr. Gary Klein secured a research grant from the U.S. Army to investigate how people make life-and-death decisions under conditions of time constraints, uncertainty and high stakes. He chose to conduct his research with fire department incident commanders (ICs) because their work met these parameters. His findings were later published in his 1998 book *Sources of Power: How People Make Decisions*, detailing operational decision-making processes.

Dr. Klein discovered that conventional decision models — typically involving evaluating multiple options to select the best outcome — did not accurately reflect how operational decisions were made in the fire service. To understand these deeper thought processes that influenced tactical choices for each event, Dr. Klein developed a cognitive interviewing process. This is crucial for us to consider, because if we can understand why firefighters take specific actions it will help us comprehend what context is driving behaviors during critical events. Later in the book we will discuss using the OODA loop in reverse when interviewing personnel. Sounds weird but stay tuned.

Klein's research identified that an incident commander's experience enables them to quickly assess an incident and act. This involves using patterns learned over time (intuition). These patterns allow ICs to envision what might or might not work, rapidly distinguishing important information from irrelevant details, anticipating outcomes of operational efforts, and responding effectively if expectations are not met. Familiar patterns help identify goals and the necessary courses of action to achieve objectives.

Experienced ICs make rapid on-the-fly decisions about initial actions based on available information. This is not a comparison of options but rather an imaginative projection of actions and their likely unfolding in the current situation. This process of imagining and acting is termed Recognition-Primed Decision-Making (RPDM). Essentially, at emergent events ICs quickly and subconsciously access a repertoire of solutions stored from their experiences, selecting the first one that appears workable. Everyone is primed at various experiential levels to recognize problem situations, which is a precursor to being recognition primed. The ability to recognize something is our level of intuition. This pattern-matching part of the process is subconscious. We are not consciously aware of matching one pattern over another.

As we imagine the outcome of a workable solution, we are consciously analyzing how things will coalesce or not. We either proceed with the first solution or move on to another. This is decision-making under the RPDM model as illustrated by the following Laundry Chute example. There is rarely time to evaluate all possible solutions and choose the absolute best one.

> Laundry Chute
> Taken from *Sources of Power,* (1998) pg. 16.
> Example 3.1
>
> The initial report describes flames in the basement of a four-story apartment building, a one-alarm fire. The commander arrives quickly but sees nothing — no signs of smoke anywhere. He locates the basement door on the side of the building, enters, and observes flames spreading up the laundry chute. It's a simple vertical fire, expected to spread straight up. Since there are no external smoke signs, it must be newly started.
>
> The strategy for a vertical fire is to get above it and spray water down. He dispatches one crew to the first floor and another to the second. Both report the fire is past them. The commander exits and walks to the building's front, where he now sees smoke emerging from under the roof's eaves. The situation is clear: the fire traveled directly to the 4th floor, hit the ceiling, and is now pushing smoke down the hall. Given no smoke was visible just a minute earlier, this must have just occurred.
>
> It is now obvious to him how to proceed, as the chance for a quick extinguishment is gone. He switches to search and rescue, prioritizing evacuation, and calls for a second alarm. The side staircase near the laundry chute, previously the focus, gives way to the front stairway as the primary evacuation route.

To conclude this subsection, let me briefly discuss the distinction between experience and expertise. For some members of the fire service, achieving expertise — the level where we understand the limitations and applications of our lived experiences as patterns — can be challenging. When we lack the direction to reflect on our successes and failures, especially through interaction with others in our field (e.g., mentor relationships), we miss opportunities to develop true expertise. Experience without meaningful or intentional reflection rarely develops into expertise. For instance, a musician without early instruction and performance in front of a host of educators, instructors and other more accomplished musicians rarely, if ever, will become an expert in their craft.

A relevant example is the 2010-2013 shift from legacy firefighting to modern fire firefighting where we learned that modern fires burn hotter, faster, and become air limited more quickly. Applying a 1.5-inch or 1.75-inch line to modern fires can be counterproductive if we fail to observe the quantity and type of fire products being consumed. Many crews habitually (mostly due to training) deploy small-diameter lines for every scenario. This pattern of quick deployment of a smaller-diameter line with lower GPM has limitations. If we fail to recognize this due to a lack of reflection, we end up gaining years of experience without developing expertise.

I advocate for both formal and informal reviews because it helps to build member expertise through larger open and formal mentoring efforts, which is a prerequisite for organizational reliability and resilience. Klein's research challenges us all to reevaluate how we train and prepare to make split second decisions on the fire ground.

High-Profile Organizational Failure

In 1986 following the Space Shuttle Challenger explosion the Rogers Commission reviewed and reported on the event concluding that the decision to launch was flawed. The Rogers Commission identified the failure of the rocket booster joint seal as the direct physical cause. However, the report also highlighted systemic organizational failures that contributed to the catastrophic event. The Commission report explicitly stated, "If those making the launch decision had known all the facts, it is highly unlikely that they would have decided to launch."[10]

87 missions later, the Space Shuttle Columbia broke apart upon reentry in January 2003.

NASA implemented numerous management reforms after the Challenger accident in 1986, but these did not adequately address the external pressures on the organization. Budget cutbacks weakened NASA's safety department. According to the Columbia investigative report in 2003 production goals and pressures began to dominate the culture, encouraging narratives of success without objective research or testing. A close observer of NASA's organizational culture noted, "cultural norms tend to be resilient. ... they bounce back into shape after being bent or stretched."[11]

---

[10] Columbia Accident Investigation Board Report Excerpts, https://www.space.com/19475-space-shuttle-columbia-disaster-investigation-report.html, 1/28/2013

[11] Ibid

1986 Challenger Explosion

Do fire service professionals believe this holds true for the fire service? A catastrophe occurs, then months or years later old habits resurface. We reacquaint ourselves with them and grow comfortable, then soon we find ourselves in the old routine(s). This is a not so helpful kind of cultural resilience.

Diane Vaughan, in her book *The Challenger Launch Decision,* corroborated these cultural observations. She cited a recorded conference call from the night before the launch revealing that NASA was aware of the risks associated with O-ring joint seal erosion. It was a known fact among all on the call that O-rings were less reliable in cold environments. Vaughan essentially linked how organizational cultural practices normalized deviations from the original understanding that the shuttle remained an experimental aircraft program.[12]

Scott Snook, in his book *Friendly Fire,* which details the downing of two U.S. Army Black Hawk helicopters by two U.S. Air Force F-15 fighters over northern Iraq on April 14, 1994, described a similar organizational characteristic he termed practical drift. His research into the shoot-down explained practical drift as a "seductive persistence of pragmatic practices loosening the grip of even the most rational and well-designed formal procedures. He further suggested that practical drift emerges when, "after extended periods of time, locally practical actions within subgroups gradually drift away from originally established procedures; those conservatively written rules

---

[12] *The Challenger Launch Decision: Risky Technology, Culture, and Deviance at NASA*, D. Vaughan, University of Chicago Press, Illinois, 1997.

designed to handle the worst-case conditions when subunits are tightly coupled. Practical drift is defined as the "slow steady uncoupling of practice from written procedure."[13]

The 2003 Columbia Accident Investigation Board (CAIB) extensively reviewed social science literature on accidents and risk, gaining insights from experts in high reliability, accident theory, and organizational safety. Chapter seven of the CAIB report introduced an interesting concept among others, a bulleted point titled "Conditioned by Success" stating: "Even after it was clear from the (earlier) launch videos that foam had struck the Orbiter in a manner never before seen, Space Shuttle Program managers were not unduly alarmed. They could not imagine why anyone would want a photo of something that could be fixed after landing." More critically, ingrained attitudes about foam strikes diminished management's awareness of their danger. The Shuttle Program transformed "the experience of failure (foam strikes) into the memory of success."

Managers also neglected to develop simple contingency plans for a reentry emergency. They were convinced, without proper study, that nothing could be done about such an emergency. The intellectual curiosity and skepticism essential for a robust safety culture was almost entirely absent. Shuttle managers did not embrace safety-conscious attitudes. Instead, their attitudes were shaped and reinforced by an organization that, in this instance, "…was incapable of stepping back and gauging its biases. Bureaucracy and process trumped thoroughness and reason."[14]

Successful operations coupled with NASA director Dan Goldin's "faster, better, cheaper" (FBC) approach fueled optimism about the shuttle program's capabilities. Due to failures in the Mars robotic program and anomalies in prior Columbia missions, the Shuttle Independent Assessment Team (SIAT) was formed to report on NASA's increasing failures. SIAT warned that the erosion of key defenses "stemming from declining staffing dedicated to safety, led to a culture increasingly reliant on safety optimism born from performance success."[15] Again, I ask, could this be true for the fire service in your region?

In chapter three of *Organization at The Limit*, Diane Vaughan highlights how the CAIB noticed strong parallels between Columbia and Challenger. Consequently, the CAIB report departed from common investigative tradition to emphasize social characteristics that influenced culture. Vaughan notes,

> "The CAIB report presented an expanded causal model that was a complete break with accident investigation tradition. The report fully embraced an organizational systems

---

[13] *Friendly Fire, The Accidental Shootdown of U.S. Black Hawks Over Northern Iraq*, Princeton University Press, New Jersey, 2000, pg. 194

[14] *Organization at the Limit: Lessons from the Columbia Disaster*, W. Starbuck, M. Farjoun, Wiley-Blackwell, New Jersey, 2005, pg.33.

[15] Columbia Accident Investigation Board, National Aeronautics and Space Administration and the Government Printing Office, Washington D.C. 2003, pg. 363

approach and was replete with social science concepts. In the Executive Summary, the report articulated both a technical cause statement and an organizational cause statement. On the latter, the board stated that it places as much weight on causal factors as on the more easily understood and corrected physical cause of the accident."[16]

Bang! There it is! The realization that the social aspects of the organization can be as causal as the technical or physical factors. This is profoundly important. While everyone refers to safety culture as part of the problem, reports rarely identify how culture played a role—only that it was involved.

As social sciences have gained more credibility in accident causation it has become increasingly evident that the past and present actions of leaders in high-risk organizations significantly influence human performance and behavior. It should no longer be easy to place blame solely on operators. We must look further into organizational causation.

> "The organizational causes of this accident are rooted in the Space Shuttle Program's history and culture, including the original compromises required to gain approval for the shuttle, subsequent years of resource constraints, fluctuating priorities, schedule pressures, mischaracterization of the shuttle as operational rather than developmental, and lack of an agreed national vision for human space flight. Cultural traits and organizational practices detrimental to safety were allowed to develop, including reliance on past success as a substitute for sound engineering practices (such as testing to understand why systems were not performing in accordance with requirements); organizational barriers that prevented effective communication of critical safety information and stifled professional differences of opinion; lack of integrated management across program elements; and the evolution of an informal chain of command and decision-making processes that operated outside the organization's rules."[17]

High-profile accidents have expanded our understanding of accident causation over the last three decades of the 20th century and into the first two decades of the 21st. Due to the interplay of multiple technologies, compressed time frames, and the endless variability of environments, review work has evolved to consider influential contextual factors — social, psychological, organizational, and technical — when determining how to conduct future operations.

---

[16] *Organization at the Limit: Lessons from the Columbia Disaster*, W. Starbuck, M. Farjoun, Wiley-Blackwell, New Jersey, 2005, pg.49.

[17] Columbia Accident Investigation Board, National Aeronautics and Space Administration and the Government Printing Office, Washington D.C. 2003, pg. 9

Section One Summation

Historical influences shape how we understand and approach accident causation today. We are products of our historical environments as well as those that currently surround us. Environments, more than anything else, influence behavior. I cannot emphasize this enough. History, traditions, beliefs, and norms all impact our decisions and responses to accidents as well as how we learn from them. Often our responses are ineffective because we revert to old familiar behaviors of blame and shame. We end up retraining only the individuals involved under the misguided belief that human behaviors can be controlled while operating in increasingly complex work environments.

Atonement rituals and scapegoating, though more elaborate today, result in less organizational learning. We are all tempted to succumb to the illusion of regaining control, believing that everything will be fine once we locate and deal with the bad apple(s). Resisting the temptation to blame is the responsibility of all Chief Officers, Captains/Supervisors, and ultimately every member of the organization. How will the fire service evolve if we don't?

As commerce industrialized and handled products on a larger scale, loss naturally grew and became more severe. Failures of ships, mining operations, bridges, and railways resulted in large-scale accidents that had a regional impact on whole communities, which included worker fatalities and permanent disabilities. Due to societal outrage, workers' compensation was founded and offered to families experiencing loss. Additionally, the AFL-CIO was formed in 1918 to assist laborers in the fight for wage protections and benefits including protection from loss due to injury, disability, and death. These societal and economic changes created laws and new administrations that managed and offered more protection for workers.

Heinrich and Bird really wanted to find a way to predict and prevent accidents. But a relationship between minor and serious events doesn't exist. Research does not demonstrate this. Sprained ankles do not predict fatalities. Nothing will replace our members taking time to size up hazards, train unceasingly, wear proper PPE, work on sufficiently staffed teams, and use the right equipment with a thorough understanding of its limitations.

With the advent of more deadly and less forgiving industries (consider nuclear) human operational error could not be tolerated and needed to be managed. Sociology and psychology were tapped to help reduce adverse outcomes when humans are part of the operational equation. Researchers took deeper dives into the human-machine interface and system complexities. Investigations began to consider human performance factors in operational environments and report them as such.

Reason and Rasmussen's research illuminated many cognitive aspects of human performance. Two avenues of failure theory came into focus. I suggest that under Reason, human behavior is commonly highlighted, and under Rasmussen, system performance is commonly highlighted.

Gary Klein's research with fire department incident commanders revealed decision-making happened through discernment of familiar patterns. ICs would look for familiar patterns recognized from prior experience, which would help identify goals and courses of action needed to achieve objectives. Much of the thought process is based on imaging outcomes. Thoughts are subconscious in the early process of recognition-primed decision-making, then as outcomes begin to become evident at the scene, more analysis is done to determine what follow-up actions should be considered or used.

As higher profile events happened, investigative teams expanded to include Ph.D.'s for the social and behavioral science aspects that rightfully should be considered. Investigative results exclusive to individual, managerial, and physical findings made room to include external system and organizational findings as part of causation. The fire service is beginning to embrace context that influences decision-making. We will need more SO/HSOs with the skills to gather data, analyze it, and then determine what to do with the findings.

Questions to Consider

1. Blame:
a) Is mean and unproductive.
b) Supports the illusion of the bad apple being the problem that needs to be fixed.
c) Means we can focus on one person's behavior.
d) Is appropriate for the person who made the mistake so they can concentrate on getting better.

2. As commerce grew in the U.S.:
a) Accidents grew in size and scale.
b) Social outrage regarding worker families spawned workers' compensation policies and laws.
c) More protections for workers were created through organizations like the AFL-CIO.
d) All the above.
e) None of the above.

3. T or F: According to Klein, the conventional decision model describes how emergency response decisions are made.

4. T or F: RPDM stands for Relevance-Primed Decision-Making.

5. T or F: Your experience offers you the ability to see patterns before you make a decision.

6. T or F: You will gain expertise the more experience you have, no matter what.

7. Organizational factors like leadership, external social pressures, and factors related to _____ can be as much of an influence on worker behaviors, if not more, as rules or regulations.
a) Success

b) Culture
c) Deviation
d) Drift

8. The organization can be as causal as the _____ or _____ causes.
a) Technical, physical
b) Internal, external
c) Environmental, cultural
d) Legal, regulatory

9. James Reason found people made errors as a fact of everyday life. In his book, *Human Error*, he constructs four labels for human error that could be used to describe the causes of accidents. Match the following:

attention failures _____	a) Violations
memory failures _____	b) Mistakes
not understanding rules or having knowledge _____	c) Slips
not following known rules _____	d) Lapses

Section Two | Organizational Influences

Culture

"The most vocal challengers to most cultures are the first to be shown the door. It's in human nature to want to eliminate the most disruptive people. And it's also human nature to want to bring in more people that fit in well. Repeat these two behaviors over time and culture becomes homogeneity, even if everyone still believes the culture values diversity." – Scott Berkun

National Fallen Firefighters Memorial

Defining culture, especially safety culture, proves challenging in our U.S. safety reviews. While often described as "the way we do things" this simplistic definition hinders our ability to intentionally understand and implement cultural change. Despite widespread agreement that culture significantly impacts Line of Duty Deaths (LODDs), accidents, and injuries our collective struggle to enact meaningful cultural change remains a persistent challenge.

Like many industries, fire service agencies often see accident numbers plateau after the initial impact of behavioral-based safety programs (discussed in the next subsection). This common pattern shows an initial decline followed by a leveling off. Currently, the fire service appears to be nearing this plateau with fatality numbers averaging around 90 over the last decade (Table 1).

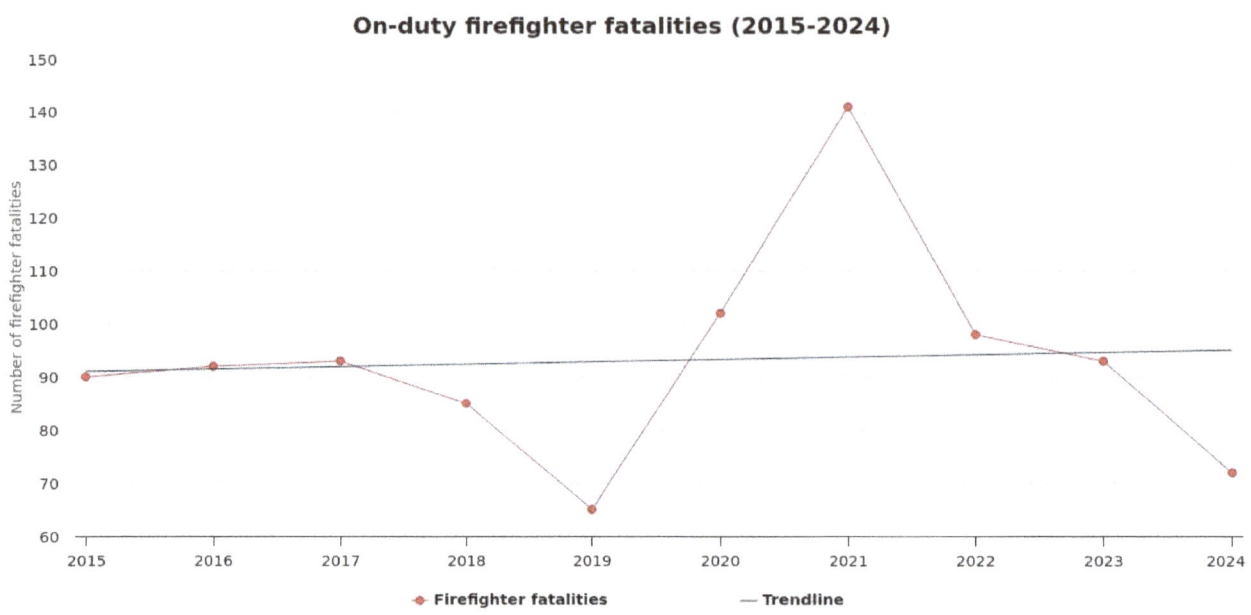

Table 1. Annual Report on Firefighter Fatalities in the United States, 2024. USFA

Measuring cultural change as both a cause and a solution for fatalities and injuries presents a significant challenge. While we intuitively grasp the significance of culture, its precise role often lacks clear explanation. We tend to believe that a better culture would have prevented LODDs or serious injuries. However, finding meaningful cultural measurements and reaching a consensus on the definition of culture or safety culture remains difficult.

Cultural surveys vary widely, assessing different aspects like artifacts, beliefs, values and sometimes deeper assumptions. If a survey aims to determine organizational alignment on issues or ensure everyone has a voice, selecting the right tool to measure collective concerns is crucial. A note of caution, however, avoid conducting surveys merely out of curiosity. Administering surveys creates an expectation that results will be transparent and lead to meaningful change if needed. A unified approach between management and labor, perhaps initiated by your department's HSO, is likely the most effective way to ensure survey results drive positive change.

Moving forward, allow me to address a commonly held belief that most Line of Duty Deaths and injuries are preventable. In hindsight, LODDs and injuries often appear preventable. Post-event, causation seems obvious because we have the time and resources to understand how various elements converged to create the outcome; information unavailable to those involved at the time. This subtly leads us to believe that different decisions or actions by specific individuals would have altered the outcome. As a result, reports often conclude, "this accident was preventable," supported by numerous counterfactual statements. *

The fundamental issue is that we simply cannot prevent every accident. This isn't pessimism; it's reality. Neither you nor I possess the ability to predict the future, so presuming we can prevent every negative outcome creates expectations that often saddle our firefighters with human error narratives that hinder true learning. Consider how someone feels or processes a finding that states they should have prevented an adverse event. In my experience, such findings are rarely helpful and hinder future cooperation when looking for solutions.

Those of us observing an event post-event on the timeline will identify numerous preventable measures, see with 20/20 vision, and have ample time to evaluate the situation — all in retrospect. Decisions and alternatives appear clear — in retrospect. However, firefighters and staff making decisions in the moment lack the clarity, time, and visible choices that retrospect offers. "In the wild," everything unfolds in real-time without access to all information. The problem arises when we forget that the review of decisions and actions benefits from full information, which is then unfairly compared to "in the wild" decisions made under severe informational and time constraints. To suggest the event was preventable adds insult to injury.

The cultural issue regarding LODDs and serious injuries isn't that culture somehow hinders preventability or that a poor culture increases probability. Rather, I believe it's about how individual and group culture necessarily influences operators within the same organization, creating conflicting interpretations, priorities, and leading to various viewpoints of the same event. We simply don't perceive things identically.

Let's illustrate:

> An apparatus operator is driving their crew to a reported working fire. The operator is speeding (well over 10 mph above the posted limit), rolling through stop signs, and cornering hard, causing significant sway. Two firefighters (FF-A and FF-B) are belted in the jump seats, donning their turnouts. FF-A is concerned about the operator's driving but is unwilling to openly challenge the driver, culturally prioritizing relational harmony. FF-B is also uncomfortable but, due to a learned cultural expectation to follow the chain of command, defers to the company officer, who is currently holding onto an overhead stability bar and the computer terminal. The company officer notices the SOP violations but weighs the risks against the rare prospect of being first to the fire — a desired firefighting experience for the team. To maintain focus and crew integrity, they decide not to intervene, being only half a mile from the address. The cultural assumption is to avoid being a buzzkill and use geographical advantage over other responding units when it is available.

*Counterfactuals are statements often preceded by phrases like "should have considered," "would have known," or "could have avoided. They create _imaginary_ alternate scenarios that are unhelpful when seeking to learn from an adverse event.

However, post-fire, the BC, who also witnessed their speed at an intersection, considers checking the engine's speed via the AVL system but chooses not to, as the fire operation went so well. Addressing this, the BC knows, would negatively impact morale, a value the department's culture wants to protect.

The Fire Chief listened to the radio, felt the fire was handled well, and this operation confirmed their belief that overall operations were proceeding smoothly. Great. No need for further verification because verification by management can be viewed as micromanaging which impacts trust. On to the next task.

Everyone here values safety. Just ask them. Yet, everyone is also a product of macro (societal) shared cultural values like:
- Individual performance as a primary value.
- Achieving goals, winning, and accepting risks.
- Respecting authority and the chain of command.

And they learn micro (organizational) shared cultural values like:
- Getting along with peers is paramount.
- Giving consideration for morale and trust because it is hard to rebuild.
- A belief that things are going well supplants the need for verifying actual performance.

Throughout the organization, embedded and accepted shared cultural values and deeper assumptions are at play. The driver/operator didn't want to let their team down by allowing the next company to arrive first. Driver/operators commonly want to avoid that outcome. Even though the driver/operator was speeding, historically passed down, shared values — stemming from organizational and lifelong societal experiences — influenced the engine's speed through unwritten cultural assumptions, values, and beliefs, ending up as artifacts. Safety competed with these values and assumptions. This is a crucial point to understand and it is encapsulated by a phrase "safety third." If culture is going to be changed leadership must understand this concept of where the artifacts come from.

I'm not excusing behavior; I'm simply stating that cultural context influences human behavior as much as, probably more, than formal rules and regulations.

In our story, the decisions (speeding, not speaking up, lack of supervision of deviant behavior) are cultural artifacts linked to values (getting along, winning, maintaining morale). These values, in turn, are connected to deeper assumptions that must be unearthed if we hope to change our culture. Cultural assumptions like "active fires are more important than the safety of our own and the public," or "an actual fire offers the best personal and group development for our members" need to be exposed and managed by leadership if we ever hope to change assumptions (move the buoy by relocating the anchor). (See Figure 4, next page.)[18]

---

[18] Pupulidy, Ph.D. International Association of Wildland Fire, 2014. Diagram accessed online March 2025. https://www.iawfonline.org/article/recognize-error-prevent-accidents/

Additionally, departmental differences exist regarding company officer involvement. But the core point here is to highlight how shared cultural values and assumptions impact safety. Measuring safety culture is difficult because safety, as a value, constantly adjusts as it competes for priority with external and internal cultural influences. It adjusts almost minute by minute.

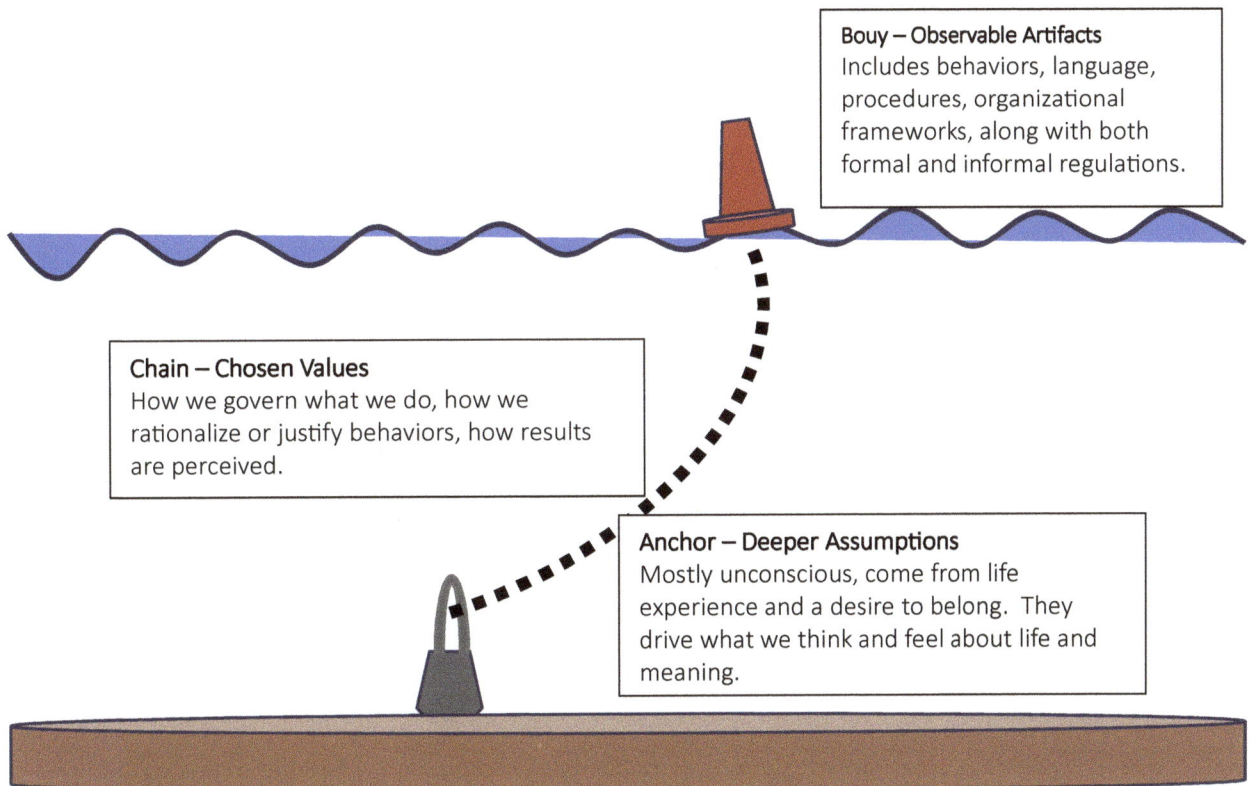

Figure 4. Buoy Culture Model. Pupulidy & Vesel (2022) Adapted from Edgar Schien

In the U.S. we profess to value <u>teamwork,</u> yet we commonly reward and discipline <u>individuals</u> for performance. Sometimes values conflict or stand paradoxically to one another. At the cultural artifact level (the easiest to evaluate) we wear uniforms to demonstrate team identity. We keep our trucks in pristine condition to show preparedness and pride. Yet, we also hold underlying assumptions (much harder to evaluate) such as it's okay to leverage the team for personal advancement and it's okay for the team to distance itself from an individual to avoid complicity when someone needs to be held accountable. This is complex. Transparency of values and assumptions is essential for any hope of changing culture's influence on behavior.

Referencing Figure 4 again, traditional human error and blame models of investigations focus resources on evaluating artifacts, learning very little about the values those artifacts were tied to. Rarely is there any effort to discover, understand and make transparent the deeper assumptions at play. This is precisely why safety culture has been so difficult to change.

As the cultural model illustration depicts, artifacts move easily (like the wind blowing on the surface) as will organizational values (bay or stream currents change daily). However, neither of them will stray far from the deeper cultural assumptions that anchor them. This implies leaders must become experts at identifying assumptions. Failing to do so means leaders will experience the resilience of how artifacts and values snap back into place around anchored assumptions resulting in no real change. Traditional investigations rarely provide leaders an opportunity to initiate fundamental change. Reviews, however, attempt to uncover and identify assumptions about work that empower leaders to move the anchor.

When I suggest we need to "Hold the Blame and Hunt to Learn" I understand it's a significant demand. Drilling down to make transparent the conflicting layers of cultural beliefs, values, and assumptions is a difficult task requiring extensive questioning of the involved members. As we hold the blame, we are more likely to look for other influential factors that will help us make sense out of what happened. A key goal of discovery phase personnel interviews is to learn and reveal the cultural context influencing behaviors. Revealing context, especially cultural assumptions, is transparency. Once we understand these contextual factors, we can challenge them or implement controls to make doing what is right easier in the future. Little is learned or gained if we simply blame or hold accountable the operator.

Effective review work should inform about contextual influences rather than highlight human error as a cause. Safety review work should make conflicting priorities transparent, thereby paving the way for firefighters to participate in building performance environments that foster resilience and greater error tolerance. If the organization merely says, "stop driving fast", we stand little chance against the underlying cultural assumptions that create the need or desire to arrive first. I believe our firefighters are intelligent individuals who genuinely want to understand the source of unspoken motivations. The why matters to them. This is forward-looking accountability; when the organization seeks to discover and share learning.

Behavioral Based Safety Efforts

Behavioral based safety (BBS) is a management methodology focused on enhancing workplace safety through direct observation and analysis of work in progress. Its primary emphasis is on fostering safe behaviors and processes among personnel. As its name suggests, BBS centers on the premise that when humans operate according to designed procedures, work is performed safely and without incident (recall James Reason's concepts of slips, lapses, mistakes, and violations from chapter one). BBS posits that safer firefighter behaviors can be influenced through encouragement, training, education, supervision, experience, or improved tools.

Following adverse events, many investigations frequently attribute causation to human error. This often leads management to intervene by seeking to dictate better work methods to prevent future incidents. Firefighters sometimes get labeled as unqualified, unmotivated, or lazy and are often excluded from intervention efforts aimed at improving work. This cycle perpetuates narratives that consistently identify human error as the cause followed by a perceived need for top-down management intervention. Consequently, genuine learning and trust-building through restorative practices becomes a lower priority, leading workers to revert to old habits of deviation, drift, and subjective optimism (more on this later).

BBS programming typically attributes errors to slips, lapses, mistakes, and violations at the component level. Components encompass technological devices, segments of work in larger processes, work procedures, training, education, tool/equipment selection, and human factors like knowledge, intelligence, situational awareness, attention span, and morale. BBS often views humans as potential liabilities or hazards due to inherent variability. Other nonhuman system components are deemed more stable unless influenced by human operation.

Investigations conducted under BBS principles frequently conclude by isolating human error as the sole cause of adverse events. The general approach involves investigating an incident, identifying unacceptable behavior, risk, or error, then redesigning processes, establishing new barriers, or retraining workers to prevent recurrence. BBS initially gained popularity in the 1960s, when work performance demands were significantly lower, and systems were "simpler and less interdependent."[19]

Human performance is often superficially diagnosed as either correct or incorrect. It appears simpler to advocate for behavioral changes as a direct route to enhanced safety, and many fire department organizations seem comfortable with this BBS approach to safety improvement. As a result of BBS, organizations have indeed seen reductions in accident and injury rates, particularly as Personal Protective Equipment (PPE) improved, operations became organized under ICS and NIMS, and essential equipment like seat belts and Self-Contained Breathing Apparatus (SCBAs) became standard. These are all positive developments. We consistently reinforced narratives and statistics that made sense to firefighters about the benefits of certain behaviors. The belief persists that this path leads to safer work. Yet, Line of Duty Deaths (LODDs) occur at ratios like decades past, and statistical improvements show some plateauing at lower levels.

When the Institute of Medicine (IOM) released their report, *To Err Is Human* (2000)[20] the public was shocked that up to 98,000 people were dying annually in hospitals due to preventable medical errors. However, as the report's title aptly implied the IOM was cautious about solely blaming healthcare professionals for mistakes. Hospitals, even with their complex organizational structures, commonly operated under BBS principles. Traditional investigations focused on identifying human error and failed

---

[19] *Safety-I to Safety-II:* A White Paper. Resilient Health Care Net: Published simultaneously by the University of Southern Denmark, University of Florida, USA, and Macquarie University, Hollnagel, Wears, and Braithwaite. Australia. 2015.

[20] Institute of Medicine (US) Committee on Quality of Health Care in America. *To Err is Human: Building a Safer Health System*. Kohn LT, Corrigan JM, Donaldson MS, editors. Washington (DC): National Academies Press (US); 2000. PMID: 25077248.

to uncover the real reasons why these errors were occurring. Human error was undeniably a factor, but as many organizations have learned over the past two decades, human error is rarely the sole reason or root cause of failures.

Regrettably, we are a fallible species so humans making errors is, well, quite normal. It's often the most boring finding of any investigation. The critical takeaway is that in today's complex work environments failure typically stems from a combination of factors beyond just human error. As the IOM report detailed, pressures from time constraints, reduced staffing, procedural changes, technological advancements, legislation, regulations, and financial and production demands all influenced the quality of care.

These factors interacted, creating a network of influences that ultimately resulted in error. Modern fire agencies are increasingly reliant on interagency dependencies, shared technology, and mutual/auto-aid agreements to address staffing needs. With tighter fiscal resources, our firefighters face growing goal conflicts (production, fiscal, safety) amid conditions of volatility, uncertainty, complexity, and ambiguity (VUCA). Effective modern safety investigative techniques and subsequent improvements will demand a thorough consideration of the context surrounding firefighter work environments and how they adapt to new realities. Unfortunately, we risk stagnation by clinging to familiar less thorough approaches, ignoring current research and continuing to use BBS principles to instruct firefighters to be more careful, more situationally aware, or less complacent. What is truly needed is a broader review framework that encompasses entire systems and the inherent complexity within them.

BBS investigations tend to emphasize identifying failures and risks then seek top-down solutions to prevent similar occurrences. Generally, the belief is that adverse outcomes result from something going wrong due to an unidentified risk or human error. Even in complex organizational investigations there's a tendency to believe that causation can be pinpointed and fixed. Effective review work should deepen our understanding of influential performance factors by comprehending how a firefighter's perspective and goals shaped their decision-making.

Human Organizational Performance

If organizational leadership and labor agree to prioritize learning over blame, it is helpful to adopt strategies and tactics related to human organizational performance (HOP).

HOP is science based with an emphasis on understanding how humans perform within organizational systems while meeting expectations set by leaders. HOP accepts human error as normal, supports processing error effectively, and encourages leaders to move systems toward error tolerance or resilience instead of impossible error-free environments. HOP is also an operational philosophy that believes individual behavior is influenced by organizational culture, processes, systems, environments, and experience. Overall HOP as a philosophy advocates for us to expect error and continually strive to understand work context, then change the system influences.

HOP supports investigative questions that shift away from who failed, to how the context surrounding decisions influenced success or failure. There are several commonly cited HOP principles:

1) **People make mistakes – Error is normal; it is not a choice.**
   - All work needs system design that can experience error and limit adverse outcomes to a minimal effect.
   - Mistakes come from how our mind handles information, not from being dumb or careless.
   - Bad things don't just happen to bad people. Bad things happen to anyone doing the work.
   - More experienced people have more skills that help them recover earlier from their mistakes.
   - If work complexity increases, errors will most likely increase as well.

2) **Blame and/or punishment fixes nothing – Leadership and labor must hold all judgment and comments that lead to or sound like scapegoating.**
   - Blame will betray trust-building efforts.
   - Blame will cut off communication efforts and access to information.
   - Blame will stifle learning and improvement efforts.
   - You can either blame and punish or learn and improve; you cannot do both.

3) **Work context drives behavior – The goal in a review is to discern what is influencing behaviors versus what is causal.**
   - Fatigue, cognitive overload, high call volume, out-of-service equipment, time pressures, and how each firefighter perceives risk differently are examples of contextual influences that might be identified.
   - Processes, pressures, values, and systems (consider ICS) drive actions and behaviors.
   - It is a goal to make future work easy to do right and hard or impossible to do wrong.
   - It's easier to change a work environment to get desired behaviors than it is to change the minds of individuals. Environment is a key influence of behavior.
   - Local rationality means people will do what makes sense to them at the time, given the circumstances. A good review identifies how firefighters made sense out of the environment they were in.

4) **Learning and improving is vital – The goal of reviewing failure and success is to prevent future harm through sharing information and making complex relationships and uncertainty in the system transparent to everyone.**
   - Learn about what and why it happened, analyze it, then embark on changes or improvements.
   - Use other similarly tasked firefighters or civilians to help analyze events. Diversity of membership on the review team helps build more meaningful interpretations post-analysis.
   - All organizational levels are learning; it is not exclusive to just one.
   - High reliability organizations are obsessed with learning and not accepting the status quo.

5) **How leaders respond to failure matters – Failure is either seen as an opportunity to learn and improve or a way to shame, blame, or retrain the "bad apple."**
   - Beware of bias, especially hindsight bias that is always 20/20. Because reviews are performed post-event, bias enters considerations because the reviewer has access to information that the people functioning in the event didn't have. Post-event bias (i.e., hindsight bias) will influence judgment and diminish curiosity of the pre-event context. Keep your opinions to yourself and be aware you will have bias, so don't sweat it, but hold them in check. Be curious.
   - Everyone has a perspective. The fact that all leaders have their own perspective means they can or may lack access to the person's perspective in the event unless they humbly ask for it. Again, be curious.

When organizational leaders stop blame processes, because research proves all humans make mistakes, then the search for context surrounding events can begin. Context surrounds the work and the workers. When searching for context I recommend asking peers to help identify the meaningful contextual influences they believe were present in the event being analyzed. (Build a Network of Influences map, page 34.) I also recommend asking peers what the organization should learn from this event and use their recommendations as keynotes for reports or presentations delivered to the organization. Facilitating the review-to-learn approach will require the selection of ad hoc groups of peer members that have demonstrated expertise related to the event, fairness, humility, and a desire

to learn. For instance, if on a haz mat call an Engine company with four haz techs had a serious event, then find another engine or ladder company with four haz tech staffing to perform the peer analysis.

Without exception, excellence exists within the fire departments at which I have had the privilege of working. Firefighters have a deep understanding of their work, which is why I suggest we put it to good use. They have intimate knowledge of the work and how to optimize response efficiency, and should the need arise, most of them are willing to test pilot improvement programs to determine which systemwide processes or ideas will work best.

Both unsuccessful and successful work is useful for identifying performance-shaping factors.[21] The problems encountered, the goal and cultural conflicts managed, the workarounds employed and the adaptations that have taken place over time are all examples of performance-shaping factors. The objective of a review is to learn how decisions became the best decisions for those who made them, then disseminate the information throughout the organization. Additionally, leadership's reaction matters and a response that views failure and success as an opportunity to learn is one of the best responses overall. The messaging received at the frontline is clear: learning is more important than blame.

HOP principles open the door to an approach that:
- Seeks firefighter and staff expertise to understand work context.
- Helps to understand when operations are at various capacity thresholds.
- Holds honest conversations about work struggles.
- Attempts to understand failure and success and the decision-making surrounding them.
- Considers firefighters and staff as problem solvers, not as problems to be fixed.
- Enhances what works well and removes what isn't useful anymore.

Here is a brief example.

> A rear-mount platform Ladder truck responded code three to an emergency medical call in a remote, annexed area of a city. The response was over six miles on city and county streets with stoplights at most intersections. As they approached one of the last intersections and needing to go straight the driver applied brake pressure due to a red light but could not slow the truck sufficiently and instead had to attempt a left turn due to oncoming traffic from the right with the intent to use all lanes and the dirt shoulder if

---

[21] *Human & Organizational Potential,* Pupulidy & Vesel, Dynamic Inquiry Inc., 2023.

needed. All traffic appeared to be stopped. However, a subcompact car traveling perpendicular to the ladder truck route on the driver's side, in the left lane of traffic, slowed but didn't completely stop entering the crosswalk area. The subcompact car driver was not expecting a wide elliptical left-turn maneuver by the ladder. The direction of travel caused the left rear sets of dually tires to roll up over the hood and front left fender of the car. No one was injured. (See Figure 5).

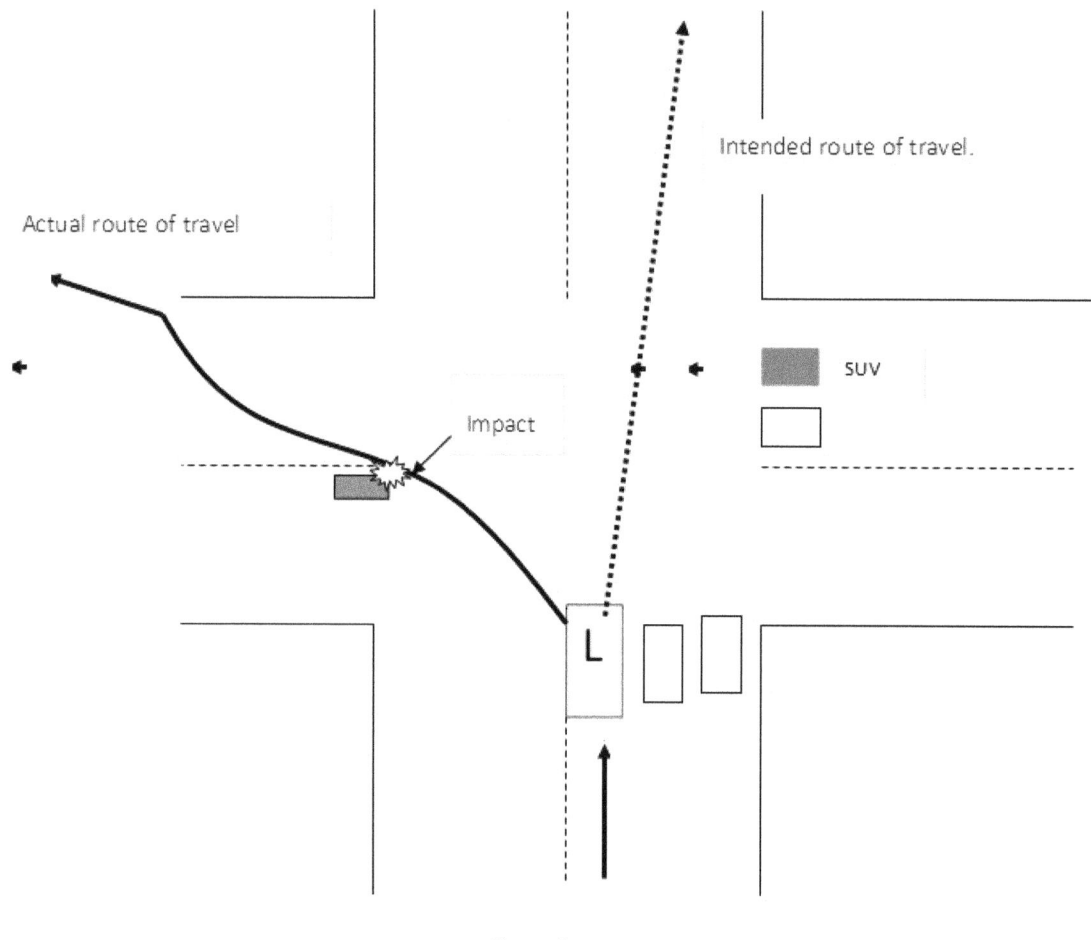

Figure 5

There were two basic choices by leadership post-event: blame or try to learn what and/or how decisions led to the accident. If we decide to hold someone accountable and blame, who will serve as the scapegoat? The ladder driver for not slowing sufficiently? The civilian car driver for not stopping and staying out of the crosswalk? Or the company officer for not preventing behaviors that led to the accident? The well-documented, poorly functioning traffic control system along the route that didn't trigger lights efficiently (or predictably) causing overuse of the brakes? Or lack of sufficient fire coverage planning for this relatively new area of the city?

If learning is leadership's primary objective, then all context is considered, especially in close calls or serious events. Once context (performance-shaping factors) is understood, learning can begin.

Here are some of the findings from this event:
- Two county-controlled flashing stoplights on the route to this area are intersections that may never have a fire department traffic control device due to jurisdictional controls, which means continued stopping at those two intersections. Therefore, all apparatus drivers should plan to make complete stops at these intersections.
- Fire department response time averages for this station should be adjusted to compensate for extended response times in the newly annexed areas of the city. Time record efficiency shouldn't reflect unchangeable conditions, like extended distances when compared to other regions with much smaller response districts.
- Mechanics have a chance to create a presentation explaining how brakes "glaze" on long runs with heavy brake use.
- Continued messaging about the uncertainties of civilian driver behavior that was encountered along the route.
- Continued messaging about goal conflict and pressures (response time averages and the driver's role vs. safety) when driving apparatus. Less emphasis on response times while enroute and more emphasis on station turnout times.
- Investigate and consider having additional internal control with an LED rear-facing monitor showing apparatus speeds to improve awareness of all on board as they assist with all eyes on the road.

There is more, but I hope you are getting the point. We can't shield this driver from a ticket resulting from an unsafe turn, but we can acknowledge the contextual influences of the driver's behaviors by improving knowledge about apparatus limitations and transparency about political factors pertaining to growth regions of the city. In addition, changing leadership expectations about response times toward manageable turnout times is essential. We must assume this can happen anywhere in the organization so efforts should be made to reduce goal conflict (production vs. safety), reset realistic expectations about what the future holds for routes into this area of the city and, if they can be identified, implement system controls that would make apparatus drivers more reliable when managing apparatus.

Leadership's response is a major factor in determining whether the organization will learn and improve or blame and punish. Messaging that the organization is more interested in learning versus blaming/punishing no matter what the event outcome is of vital importance. I'm sure this driver feels bad enough about the mistake, the damage, and the extended response time for this call.

If this type of practice is not a familiar expectation in your fire department, then your department will remain vulnerable to using retributive practices that only attempt to secure the illusion that you can get rid of or retrain the bad apple. Nothing will change except morale and the willingness to openly share with leadership. Start now establishing a history of dealing with error events with an emphasis on learning. Form a committee, look at policies and procedures, make new ones that include language that affirms the desire to learn, and have leadership sign off on them as a new beginning.

Author Todd Conklin, Ph.D., offers several questions that help start the task of conducting a post-event review in the direction of learning. I have paraphrased some of them here.[22]

- Are the people okay?
- Is everything else secure and stable?
- Tell me the story of what happened.
- What else could have happened that might have been worse?
- What are the important factors as you understand them that led to this event?
- What worked as it should? What didn't work well?
- Where else could this happen in our organization?
- What else can you tell us about this event that we need to know?

I found safety management in the fire service to be a natural fit for HOP principles. Everyone understands our calls contain variability, uncertainty, complexity, and ambiguity (VUCA). The tendency, although not universal, is to give our brothers and sisters who make mistakes the benefit of the doubt. If leadership supports HOP principles, learning reviews can uncover context related to past and future practices and unknown goal conflicts where the work gets done.

Complex Systems

"Underneath every simple, obvious story about 'human error' there is a deeper, more complex story about the organization." – Sidney Dekker

Before we define complexity, let's take a moment to describe system types that we will encounter when considering reviews.

It's easy to look at something like your basic bicycle and see that it is a simple system. You get on it, use the handles to steer it, and propel it with your legs and feet, moving the pedals in a circular motion where the chain is geared to the rear wheel and the bicycle is propelled forward. If the chain breaks, the system no longer works. This is a simple cause-and-effect relationship, and it can be graphed in a linear timeline fashion. The solution is simple and once the chain is fixed or replaced the system works again.

A complicated system could be something like a small airplane. It is made up of numerous cause-and-effect relationships that work together to provide the function of flight. The engine and propeller propel the aircraft forward. The wings and flaps create lift so the aircraft can fly. Numerous other systems are employed to control, communicate, and inform the pilot about how all the systems are functioning. The environment, which at times is unpredictable, influences flight. Should something

---

[22] *Pre-Accident Investigations, An Introduction to Organizational Safety,* T. Conklin, Ashgate Publishing, Surrey England, 2012. Pg. 40.

break, the other systems may help with flight for a short period of time but eventually the system cannot perform the function of flight, and gravity wins.

Complex systems, like fire departments, are made up of numerous systems that interact, providing the outcomes of emergency response, prevention, public education, and support services. All fire department outcomes are influenced by global and local politics, finances, legal entities, and administrative rules or regulations. Often, the interactions between any of these systems or influences are unknown or remain hidden until something happens and the weaknesses are exposed. If a fire department commonly runs with 3-person staffing, and for one-half day they run with two and that unit is first due on a fire call where only one person makes entry to extinguish the flames, a weakness is exposed regardless of the complex relationships that created it.

When conducting reviews where equipment failed, consider whether it is a simple system failure or a complicated system failure, and consider creating a linear diagram that highlights the story of the failure. If time was an important factor, then add that to the diagram, but only if it was an important factor.

Complexity and the decision-making we are trying to understand is harder to diagram. This usually involves several factors (personal and organizational) that interact under VUCA circumstances. Decision-making in complex environments does not lend itself to linear diagraming (Figure 6) because we are trying to understand influences and conditions that led to decision-making in the moment (sensemaking). Influence and decision-making context are not the same as determining cause and effect. This is a different accident model. Be sure you understand which type of system you are trying to review.

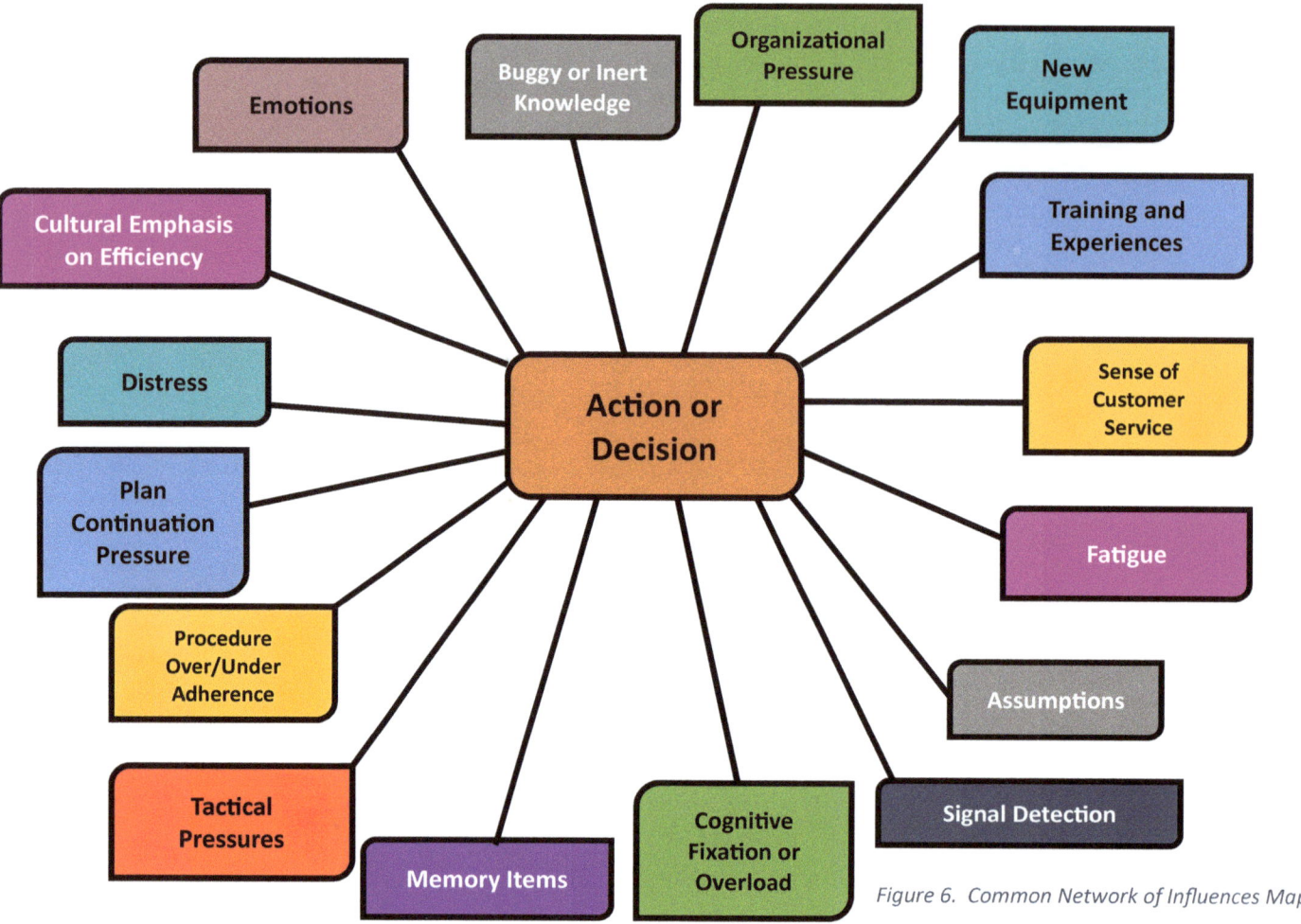

Figure 6. Common Network of Influences Map

Additionally, complexity can contain the characteristic of relational "coupling" (tight or loose) between known and unknown external and internal parts that are continually interacting. Consider how apparatus maintenance and frontline drivers must work together to keep apparatus ready, or the many hardware and software components of information processing systems like fire technical services and dispatch systems that need to feed reliable information to frontline crews. Simply stated, coupling is about how time or relationships and their disruptions will increase or decrease the chances of loss.

Water supply at a working fire is a good example of complexity with tight coupling. It doesn't tolerate delay. When fire hydrants are the primary source of water there is a very limited buffer (tank water) in the event the hydrant does not work. However, a fire inspection is an example of complexity with loose coupling. Delays getting it done are easily recoverable.[23]

Review work that exposes complex, hidden relationships will offer organizations the ability to manage relationships that can have serious consequences on operations. These are significant learning opportunities for all organizations. Tightly coupled complex relationships need to be identified within

---

[23] *Normal Accidents, Living with High-Risk Technologies*, C. Perrow, Princeton University Press, New Jersey, 1999

every division and made known to all department members. Awareness across divisions elevates everyone's understanding of how work is interdependent and connected.

An example of fire department complexity and coupling was the PPE shortages at the onset of the COVID-19 pandemic. Complex system factors like staffing positions that were essential, changing guidelines, sudden demands for treatment changes, and supply disruptions were experienced like waves on the beach. At times, especially in the beginning of the pandemic, coupling became tight, where earlier it was loose. Political, medical sources, and governing groups updated information sometimes two or three times a day. We were all caught off guard by our interdependencies and the duty to act cooperatively.

Complexity impacts organizational safety, reliability, and resilience because we often don't clearly see the internal or external organizational coupling that can impact the organization. Performance can be difficult when we are surprised by operations that are related or interdependent. Complexity is metaphorically more like an asymmetrical spiderweb than a symmetrical linear flow chart. Pulling on one strand of the web creates tension on several other strands and changes the web design, depending on what new strands are interwoven from day to day. The web still must complete its function.

Asymmetrical Web

Be grateful when frontline workers (mechanics, technical workers, dispatchers, medical oversight, training staff, administrators, and firefighters) adapt, compensate, and generally get things done. If your department is flexible and absorbs stressors most of the time, it is usually because your members adjusted and still completed the work. The same people we may think are unreliable and make poor judgment calls are the same people who add necessary flexibility to our response systems. Good review work will uncover their resilience, even in operations with failure.

Reliability and Resilience

"We want resilience in our systems, so we design for reliability." – Richard Cook

Simply stated, resilience and reliability are defined as:
  Reliability: The consistent ability to perform well.
  Resilience: The capacity to quickly recover from difficulties or adapt to change.

In other words, to effectively bounce back from the unexpected we must design our systems for consistent performance, then rigorously test them for strength and flexibility. Achieving consistent reliability is a significant challenge. In emergency services we rely on established protocols like Airway, Breathing, Circulation, Disability (ABCD) for EMS calls, and employ risk-benefit analyses in rescue situations. Order models are complemented by training that enables professionals to differentiate between serious and minor issues. As EMTs and paramedics gain experience they operate more consistently within these medical control models, thereby increasing the medical system's reliability. This, in turn, fosters resilience, allowing the system to recover and adapt when faced with high-demand situations like multiple patient incidents.

Interestingly, achieving reliability seems increasingly difficult given the fire service's ever-expanding all-hazards mission. It sometimes feels as though we might be compromising our desire to be reliable as we pursue mission relevance. Here are some examples:
- In the late 1960s and 1970s, the fire service integrated Vietnam medic programs, leading to the establishment of prehospital paramedic services in the U.S.
- The 1980s saw the adoption of DOT guidelines and the development of advanced Hazardous Materials teams, driven by the increased prevalence of hazardous material transport.
- Throughout the 1990s, the concept of "mission expansion" continued, fostering the growth of various technical rescue disciplines.
- Post-2001, the implementation of NIMS (National Incident Management System) and the expansion of heavy rescue capabilities emerged as a response to terrorism threats.
- Around 2010, community paramedicine initiatives aimed to reduce costs and address the rising demand for nonemergent public health issues, including behavioral health.

Clearly, the fire service has a long history of developing new programs to maintain its relevance to the public. However, departments often pursue mission areas they may not be fully equipped to support. The absence of catastrophic events is not a reliable indicator of safety performance.

For instance, staffing levels — such as reductions from 4 to 3, or 3 to 2, whether referring to personnel or those with specialty certifications — on an Engine or Ladder company can significantly impact an organization's reliability and resilience. From a planned reliability perspective, specific call types demand certain minimum staffing levels. For instance, technical rescue specialty units should be dispatched concurrently with a confined space rescue call to enhance reliability from a staffing standpoint.

Operational resilience is inherently compromised if reliability standards are not firmly established. With the deployment of adequately trained resources success becomes more probable and failures are less likely to be severe, as VUCA factors are more likely to be identified early and managed effectively with sufficient personnel on hand.

Staffing reliability, which demands adequate capacity, provides the foundation for resilience. While not a foolproof plan, it significantly improves the chances of successful outcomes. Predetermined staffing capacity introduces strength and flexibility (alternative options) into any incident command system operating in response mode. Because VUCA is a common reality, our systems must rely on fundamental elements like adequate staffing. This is intuitively understood, and data consistently supports it. Yet, many departments feel compelled to operate with fewer resources to remain fiscally viable while their policymakers, as well as the public, are unaware of the developing tension. This "doing more with less" mentality can even become a source of bravado, which, arguably, compromises professionalism and safety.

It is concerning when reliability is evaluated solely as an outcome (typically after a failed event) rather than as a crucial input. This approach undermines community trust and confidence in an organization's ability to perform. The long-term objective for reliability should be continuous improvement, never being satisfied with the current level. Always strive for the next level, not just in staffing, but also in training, competency requirements, equipment, and operational systems. As you strategically build, train, and adapt for reliability, resilience naturally develops, leading to less severe adverse operational outcomes.

One of the most effective ways to practice system resilience is by continuously monitoring and measuring essential characteristics, often referred to as the four cornerstones of resilience: respond, monitor, anticipate, and learn. Defined more fully, system resilience means: "The system must be able to respond to any type of event (addressing the actual), monitor underway evolutions (addressing the critical), anticipate future threats and opportunities (addressing the potential), and learn from past failures and successes (addressing the factual)."[24]

Developing metrics for these resilience cornerstones provides a framework for assessing an organization's resilience potential and identifying areas needing improvement. When analyzing events, efforts should be made to examine the following:
- Identifying existing or missing capacities crucial for an effective response to the event under review.
- Defining all relevant indicators that provided insight into the working conditions.
- Assessing whether those involved were able to detect threats promptly, efficiently, and with increasing preparedness.
- Determining if there were reasonable past opportunities to learn from similar situations and whether those lessons were successfully integrated.

It is crucial to remember that resilience is both a systemic and individual characteristic. To elaborate, resilience is a system's and an individual's ability "to recognize, absorb, or adapt to harmful influences."[25] This includes capacities such as "anticipating, monitoring, responding, and learning."[26]

Restorative Practice

"The things we fear most in organizations — fluctuations, disturbances, imbalances — are the primary sources of creativity." – Margaret J. Wheatley

Leadership should consider how they respond to error events making commitments to more restorative practices in the organization. More restorative practices are finding their way into all kinds of industries and organizations. Restoration in organizations has other names like restorative just culture, restorative just theory, restorative culture, just culture, restorative justice, and what I will use for this manuscript, restorative practice.

---

[24] Rankin A., Lundberg J., Woltjer R. A framework for learning from adaptive performance. In: Nemeth

[25] C.P., Hollnagel E., editors. Becom. *Resilient*. Ashgate Publishing, Ltd; 2014. pp. 79–96.

[26] *Compliance Capitalism: How free markets have led to unfree, overregulated workers.* S. Dekker, London: Routledge. 2022.

Chances are good your organization has some values and structure that offer support for restorative practices already. I think it would be rare to have a department that is starting from scratch. As I offer the following list of restorative practices, you might consider what makes sense for your organization.

Restorative practices include specific processes and actions that support learning for individuals and removing punitive investigative outcomes. Restorative practice attempts to value those who make mistakes (errors) and have a desire to reconcile or make recompense to those injured or to the organization. Great service delivery is performed by people who constantly learn and improve, especially after an adverse event outcome. Learning is enhanced by adhering to the restorative practices listed below: [27]

> **Inclusive Committee Work** – Labor and management should serve as co-chairs of the committee and the rest of the committee make up should be a diverse cross-section of the entire department. Don't forget to include contractors, vendors, and community input when it makes sense.
>
> **Make Doing It Right Easy** – Program, policy, procedures, and work design should be made with an emphasis on being easy to follow. For instance, if you want close calls to be reported, make the form easy to fill out (name, contact number, brief narrative). The effort to collect details should be shouldered by staff that performs close call discovery work. Maintain confidentiality when it makes sense.
>
> **Teach Psychological Safety** – When psychological safety exists members will contribute perspectives, ask questions, and offer honest opinions without the fear of embarrassment, ridicule, retribution, or having their reputation compromised. There are excellent resources that inform and teach how to manage psychological safety, starting with leadership. More on this later.
>
> **Manage Language** – When speaking or writing policies and resolutions be careful to use clear vocabulary that doesn't carry emotional charge. Agree on words in procedures as a group, not as an individual. Seek input and consensus if you are the scribe/writer.
>
> **Safety Leadership is Learned** – I haven't met a leader yet who hasn't experienced failure. Most know they need the talent, contributions, and expertise of the people surrounding them. The American myth of the self-made leader is just that, a myth. Chances are good leaders around you didn't achieve their rank or position without a few personality "tune up" moments along the way. Humble leaders understand the difference between success and failure is often about perspective, so the more perspectives we invite the better.

---

[27] *Safety-II in Practice: Developing the resilience potentials*. E. Hollnagel, London: Routledge. 2018

On a personal note, as a Battalion Chief I was overly committed to my leadership style, thoughts, and tactics. When I had success in the organization my thoughts and behaviors were affirmed. Being told by a close co-worker, "Hey maybe that's not working as well in this area of management" put me on the defensive. At first, it wasn't easy listening to constructive feedback. However, I soon found accepting constructive feedback was freedom from listening to the rather self-centered voices in my head. I started craving to hear what others thought for the remainder of my career, especially after my failures. Thank you, Kurt!

BIAS

This subsection will define bias and explain its profound effects on the analysis of serious events. To illustrate, we will delve into several biases frequently encountered by review teams and explore our initial reactions when we first learn about an event or witness it through video footage.

Bias is an inclination either for or against something; a mental pattern of distortion that shapes how we perceive people or situations. To better understand this, let's consider an adverse event. As you read the following narrative, pay close attention to your internal emotional responses. Consider noting any emotions you experience, when you find yourself making assumptions, and prioritize the most frequent feelings. I have deliberately removed names, dates, and have not referenced the news agency.

> The family of a man who died after a responder allegedly injected him with the wrong drug is suing. The lawsuit targets the city, its fire and rescue department, and the city police department in a U.S. District Court.
>
> The lawsuit claims that in the early hours of a summer night in 2023, a police officer responded to a call about a man sitting or lying along the curb of a deserted residential street. The man informed the officer he had injured his arm, eventually leading to eight responders from both the police and fire and rescue departments arriving on scene.
>
> According to the lawsuit, the young man "never posed any threat" to the responders; instead, he was disoriented and fearful, repeatedly attempting to move away from them. At one point, a fire paramedic allegedly decided the situation warranted the use of a chemical restraint, specifically, the incapacitating drug ketamine. With the assistance of other responders, the man was "held down and injected against his will." The lawsuit further states, "However, instead of injecting him with ketamine, the paramedic injected him with a lethal dose of the paralytic medication rocuronium." Body-cam footage, the lawsuit claims, shows the victim soon gasping for air and repeatedly crying, "I can't

breathe" while asking, "Am I gonna die?" One of the police officers allegedly replied, "You're not gonna die; you're fine."

The suit also alleges that "The paramedic realized that the incorrect and life-threatening medication rocuronium was given, but did not notify anyone, nor was any action taken to protect the victim's airway and/or intubate him before he became paralyzed and unable to breathe. Not a single person on-scene mentioned the male victim's objectively obvious respiratory distress. Instead, police officers handcuffed the chemically incapacitated victim and strapped him to a gurney."

Minutes later, the victim lay motionless with his eyes open, and one individual on-scene told him, "Night-night," according to the lawsuit. En route to the hospital, the victim's heart stopped, and the paramedic allegedly called ahead, falsely reporting that the victim had been given a dose of ketamine. Upon arrival at the hospital, the lawsuit alleges, the paramedic "finally informed medical personnel that the victim had been injected with rocuronium. The paramedic then continued the clumsy cover-up by improperly disposing of the vials of rocuronium and ketamine in a sharps container in contravention of the fire and rescue department's policies and procedures." The victim died two days later, allegedly from an anoxic brain injury due to the administration of rocuronium, as stated in the lawsuit.

After reading this narrative, what is your predominant emotion? Do you feel angry, shocked, disgusted, compassionate, sad, embarrassed, or do you simply want to get as far away from this story as possible? Whatever your emotion, it is crucial to recognize that what you are experiencing is called "emotional conductivity." * Whether watching body-cam footage or reading any narrative we inevitably have emotional reactions to what we are seeing, hearing, reading, or imagining. This is a normal, natural response stemming from our own learned social and emotional conditioning.

It quickly becomes clear that emotions during serious events can undermine our efforts to conduct thorough, fair, and objective event analyses. Emotional conductivity also makes it easy to connect with other biases that feel emotionally satisfying but will lack objectivity.

Emotional responses are a normal part of being human. They help us navigate the immense amount of information surrounding us at any given time. The danger here lies in failing to recognize and manage it when facilitating a review of an operational failure that leads to consequential results. What is needed, after acknowledging our emotional reaction, is a well-structured analytical review of the facts and the context surrounding the event.

---

* Emotional conductivity is the process by which emotions shape an investigator's interpretation of evidence. When watching a video, especially one involving a high-stakes incident, investigators naturally bring their past experiences, expectations, and emotional reactions to the table. These factors can create a biased lens, leading to theories based on feelings rather than facts. Borden, 2023.

If my initial emotion regarding the case above is anger, I'm more likely to prioritize information that confirms my displeasure with the paramedic's actions rather than attempting to understand the reasoning behind his/her choices. Prioritizing information that confirms our feelings and beliefs and giving that information greater weight or prematurely stopping the inquiry once preferred evidence is found is a common phenomenon known as confirmation bias.

In this adverse event, succumbing to confirmation bias would lead to selective listening, preventing us from asking interview questions that explore on-scene reasoning from firefighters and paramedics,

scene confusion, operational duty to act or pressure to perform, poor lighting, distractions, or perhaps the absence of a second paramedic who could have conducted a secondary medication check. We might also neglect to construct a more accurate and inclusive narrative relying instead solely on the plaintiff's attorney's account which is written to persuade.

Combating confirmation bias requires intentional effort. First, recognize that it is natural to take a side in any situation based on your personal assumptions and beliefs. To minimize the chances of your natural tendencies derailing a review process it is imperative to follow a structured review process making every effort to conduct thorough cognitive interviews with everyone involved. Whenever possible, employ two review facilitators to collect data, evidence, and conduct interviews. Do interviews as soon as possible after the event and ideally have one review facilitator unaware of the event's outcome to reduce the likelihood of grappling with common biases (confirmation, hindsight, outcome).

Second, it is more professional for fire department members who are not personally acquainted with those involved in the event to conduct the review's discovery and analysis phases. In fact, if trained fire department members from a neighboring organization can facilitate the review, the level of professionalism will significantly increase. This is why I believe it would be beneficial for states or regions to establish regional review teams that operate under mutual aid agreements providing review services to local fire departments or ambulance companies when requested. Why not? We do it for almost everything else. *

Another commonly experienced bias during reviews is hindsight bias. The adage, "hindsight is 20/20," refers to how looking back at an event, with knowledge of the outcome, makes it easy to judge past decisions as good or bad. The problem with hindsight bias is that decisions are evaluated based on outcomes not on the firefighter's (including all ranks) narrow focus of attention during the actual event. As reviewers, we must continually remind ourselves that we seek the perspective of those involved in the event. We must, as Sidney Dekker states, "get in the tunnel with them."[28]

* Many believe it's suboptimal for an organization to review itself after an adverse event due to unmanageable bias or fears of a cover-up. Conversely, others fear that airing their internal issues to neighboring departments would be embarrassing or diminish confidence in their organization. Building regional teams to mutual aid with each other would be an achievable model to adopt.

---

[28] Adapted from Restorative Just Culture in Practice, Dekker, Oats, and Rafferty. Routledge, New York, New York. 2022.

Unfortunately, we rarely see review findings that articulate the thoughts and feelings experienced, or that determined what was important to those making decisions at the time and why those decisions seemed correct. This overlooks how the organization or the system itself might have placed firefighters at a disadvantage or offered them limited information prior to the event. Hindsight bias subtly steers well-intentioned investigators away from the human reasons behind an incident — instead they deliver only what happened — which often boils down to some version of human error leading to blaming, shaming, and retraining.

How can we blame someone when, even for the best trained among us, stress leads to human factors like vision, hearing, and cognition naturally getting reduced and allowing the brain to process what it deems relevant at the time. Vision, which typically dominates other senses in terms of "brain bandwidth" narrows to about 3% of total visual range under duress. That is the equivalent of you holding your thumb at arm's length in front of you and visually processing, or understanding, what is behind your thumb nail! Information (data) is filtered as the brain responds and uses our senses to find critical meaningful information. It is a survival mechanism not to have to consider and process everything.

When review facilitators experience emotional conductivity and fail to manage it, they are more susceptible to biases like hindsight bias and confirmation bias. This can sabotage the review with limited examination, superficial findings, and missed organizational learning opportunities. Consequently, chances to challenge and strengthen our systems are lost.

Hindsight bias is managed similarly to confirmation bias. Part of the structured review process mentioned earlier involves the OODA loop,* which can be applied in reverse when evaluating decisions made during emergency events. Bias is better managed when we use this framework to list all **Actions** taken at an event documenting the **Decisions** made for each action, understanding the firefighter's **Orientation** to the event, and helping each participant recall what they **Observed**. A structured analysis is useful, and it can meaningfully reduce investigator bias that might otherwise limit findings.

Finally, regarding bias, we must foster diversity among review team members and provide psychologically safe environments for them to speak up. Otherwise you will most likely become a homogeneous groupthink; meaning you'll operate under similar biases and naturally exclude deeper context or cultural issues that don't fit, serving only to expedite the review process.

Bias erects barriers to learning and commonly (very commonly) results in a lack of curiosity, poor questioning, and final reports that lack narrative or a rich story to tell. I suggest we adopt a humble approach and keep reminding ourselves, "I could have done this if I were in their shoes," or acknowledge that no one can predict the future so any one of us could have faced a similar situation.

*OODA represents Observe, Orient, Decide, and Act. It was developed by Colonel John Boyd, USAF, in 1986 and was used as a faster decision model for USAF pilots who outperformed Soviet pilots in the Korean War. I learned this from a three-day class through Critical Incident Review, Sgt. Jamie Borden (Ret.). The class was about the intricacies and limitations of video evidence, but I learned much more. Borden is an amazingly talented investigator.

Here are a few common biases to watch for:

Fundamental Attribution Error Bias: This bias makes it difficult to access deeper layers of context. Fundamental attribution error is our tendency to attribute other people's actions to their personality while believing our similar actions are due to external factors beyond our control (e.g., "I wrecked the car because there were so many other cars around me; therefore, I had nowhere to go," versus "He/she wrecked the car because they are a risk-taker, careless, or inexperienced.") The problem with fundamental attribution error is that it short-circuits the desire to examine the entire system and the micro or macro cultural influences that play a role in decision-making. Simple blame of the individual making the error suffices without deeper investigation.

Social Confirmation Bias: We find it very hard to acknowledge something our group doesn't want us to see. In other words, we seek to please the group over finding the truth. This often occurs in groups that lack diversity, especially diversity of rank.

Complexity Bias: The human brain prefers simple explanations over complex truths. This can be an issue when selecting and orienting the peer team invited to conduct the analysis and sensemaking of the event. We all desire simplicity. However, an analysis can be hijacked by a strong personality unwilling to expend the energy required for thoroughness, fairness, and sometimes lengthy discussions. Prep of the peer team is essential.

Competency Bias: We tend to view ourselves as above average. It is often necessary to perceive others as incompetent to affirm our self-image. In essence, we will search for information that affirms the mistakes of others and is attributed to individuals who lack intelligence or skills.

Outcome Bias: This is the tendency to assess a decision based solely on its outcome without evaluating the decision-making process at the time the decision was made. It focuses on results not on the process and the idea that chance may have played a role is deemed irrelevant.

Numerous other biases can be described and any of them can oversimplify or hijack a review process and its outcome. Anyone facilitating reviews needs to accept and understand that bias will be present and must take concrete steps, like using the OODA loop in reverse to reduce the impact of individual and group biases. Review teams require diversity of background, thought, and experience. Homogeneous review teams often result in what I consider anemic final review findings due to unconscious biases.

Reduce Retributive Practices

For the fire service to truly learn from its mistakes and successes, leadership must champion a shift away from retributive practices. Traditional investigative approaches often:

- Focus primarily on identifying the responsible party.
- Fail to teach or value alternative behaviors and instead highlight failures and enforce stricter adherence to procedures.
- Prioritize rules over the operational context.
- Aggressively seek blame and hold individuals accountable.
- Neglect or dedicate insufficient time to understanding context.
- Rarely allow for restitution or sincere apologies from firefighters or staff who make mistakes.

Behavioral sciences provide overwhelming evidence that positive support and encouragement foster trust and a willingness to openly share challenges. Firefighters will not inherently trust that the organization supports them if past experiences reveal retributive practices. Moving towards positive support and encouragement requires leaders in both management and labor to seek training and adopt language that shifts away from error that has retributive responses.

When an organization's objective is to determine fault or cause rather than to learn or understand context something critical is overlooked. If the underlying goal is to assign blame or punish individuals for their actions, the organizational system leans towards being retributive. Systems often oscillate between retributive and restorative approaches which can vary from one chief officer to another, or day to day. We tend to mimic our society's justice systems which are predominantly retributive. This inherent nature of the societal justice system influences cultural, economic, and governmental environments, pushing organizations, including fire departments, to adopt retributive practices to avoid appearing weak or out of sync.

Our objective must be to embrace restorative practices and empower personnel to openly discuss work-related struggles and conflicts, thereby integrating them into the improvement process. This will take time as it is often not the natural inclination of firefighters or staff to see themselves as problem identifiers or solvers. Which is another reason why it is crucial to refrain from scapegoating, even when fulfilling administrative obligations to hold people accountable.

After an adverse event, most firefighters will return to work facing the same pressures and goal conflicts as before, if nothing changes. Unexamined failures persist in organizations that do not understand how to modify, control, or enhance the system — the primary influencer of behavior. Without change, the potential for catastrophic outcomes remains.

Researcher Erik Hollnagel offers a deeper understanding of the daily tension between work demands and safety as the efficiency-thoroughness trade-off (ETTO). He and his colleagues explain that "workers are as safe as they need to be without being overly safe in order to be productive." Every organization experiences this continuous ETTO tension at every moment.[29] I interpret this to mean ETTO is the normal nature of everyday work. Therefore, we should facilitate reviews that seek to understand these daily trade-offs and identify how we can consistently make safe work practices the easiest choice.

---

[29] ETTO Principle: Efficiency-Thoroughness Trade-Off: Why Things That Go Right Sometimes Go Wrong.

Ultimately, when an organization scapegoats or goes so far as to sacrifice someone's career, the remaining firefighters will revert to business as usual, completing tasks in ways that make sense to them. This occurs because no apparent organizational change has taken place, thus workers return with diminished expectations of improvement. It is worth reiterating, scapegoating perpetuates the illusion that our problems stem from individuals failing to make the right choices.

Accountability

If you're anything like me, you're starting to feel some discomfort with the idea that we're going to let firefighters making mistakes off the hook and chaos will reign. It'll become a free-for-all!

Trust me, I am not abandoning procedures, policies, or the rule of law. What I'm advocating for is more organizational accountability where, after an event, the organization is accountable for learning as much as it can to prevent the next accident.* Increased organizational accountability will require that we replace current narratives about root cause or causation with new narratives and processes that seek to understand how conditions and/or influences played a role in event decision-making.

The suggestion here is that we use reviews for the complex situations the fire service experiences. As error is found, it is used as a starting point for a review. Error is examined thoroughly, as each error has rich context and requires analysis. The facilitator's organizational objective is to make sense of the decisions made at the time. The review goal is to understand the relationship between actions and conditions. This is how the organization implements forward-looking accountability. To look back and identify blame is rear-facing accountability. As we understand what was observed by those involved and their orientation to what was taking place, including how and why they made their decisions, we will begin to understand their actions.[30]

After an Adverse Event

Restorative practice does not let people off the hook rather; it actively engages all parties involved in an adverse event. Through this process, we can address the harm caused, foster empathy for those who made errors, understand the context of why an error occurred and resolve influential systemic issues, which would facilitate restitution.

When mistakes lead to someone becoming a victim, they typically seek sincere apologies, a deep understanding of what and why it happened, and assurances that steps will be taken to prevent future

---

* Ivan Pupulidy played a key role in the U.S. Forest Service's adoption of learning reviews post adverse event, instead of conducting traditional investigations. Prior to that he was a forest service pilot, regional aviation safety manager, and a chief accident investigator. He also helped to develop the idea of forward-facing accountability for organizations versus the common rear-facing accountability we commonly experience.

[30] *Anatomy of a Critical Incident: Navigating Controversy*, Borden, Twigg PhD, et all, Independent KDP, Las Vegas NV, 2024

occurrences. This is consistently supported by research. Yet, a common counterproductive practice is to isolate individuals who commit serious errors and instruct them not to discuss the event. This isolation only compounds the trauma for those who caused harm and, in my view, creates a false sense of organizational protection from liability. It also alienates victims, families, and other affected parties. A restorative approach, conversely, offers fair restitution to those injured or suffering loss and supports

those who caused harm by integrating them into, rather than ostracizing them from their organizational support systems. As a result of the sequestering mentality, since approximately 2010, the term "second victim" has emerged to describe individuals who played a role in an error event.[31]

Restorative practice acknowledges that firefighters are more than just components of the systems they operate within. Workers contribute to system complexity by incorporating factors such as emotions, well-being, experience, and motivation, which are affected by everyday circumstances. When these factors are combined with an expectation of flawless performance under varying pressures in team operations, complexity is easier to identify as a contributing factor. It is a true testament to our training and team functions that emergency operations achieve success as often as they do.

Most of the time, the risks and VUCA inherent in fire, rescue, and medical services are managed with professionalism and care. Firefighters contend with increasing call volumes, fatigue from poor sleep, stress from dangerous calls, and ongoing training, all while balancing efficiency, production, and personal safety. When internal or external errors occur within the fire service there is rarely a specific, universally applicable restorative framework. From my experience, the most effective method involves a management-labor collaboration that establishes agreed-upon basic restorative practices.

Interestingly, organizational learning stems not only from reviewing what goes wrong, but also from analyzing what goes right. Efforts to understand why operations consistently succeed offers profound insights into an organization's reliability and resilience.

As an example, a department Safety Officer (SO) conducted a radio report audit of all working structure fire communications to identify factors consistently present during successful outcomes. Although "success" was broadly defined as "when things worked well," the audit yielded valuable insights.
One consistent discovery was that successful outcomes frequently correlated with initial arriving units completing 360-degree reports. This finding reinforced earlier policy changes that had already added 360-degree reports to the initial on-scene activities for first-arriving units. This self-audit was a relatively small, yet valuable effort that invested time in understanding success. It exemplifies how safety personnel can help an organization pursue operational efficiency and reliability; goals every department aims to demonstrate and integrate into its narrative for organizational learning.

---

[31] *Second Victim: Error, Guilt, Trauma, and Resilience*. S. Dekker. CRC Press, Boca Rotan, Florida. 2013

Section Two Summation

Identifying an organization's safety culture presents significant challenges. When blame is assigned as the primary cause for an injury accident, for instance, it often obscures or replaces systemic contributions that remain unaddressed in final reports. Culture also plays a crucial role in perpetuating internal conflicts between shared organizational values and their integration with the broader macro-culture.

For instance, cultural expectations can vary widely between a small, rural combination fire department and a larger municipal career department in the U.S. Furthermore, every individual brings a unique set of personal values and influences to daily work, impacting their decision-making. A key objective of a review is to help leadership understand their role as a cultural influencer.

Culture is inherently difficult to measure, except at the artifact level, and challenging to define without oversimplification. While safety culture receives considerable attention, there's a greater need for education on measurable indicators of its influence. The goal of improving safety culture can be elusive, as culture itself is a subjective measurement that can fluctuate daily. Assessments of cultural assumptions are key to moving culture one way or another. Focus on moving cultural assumptions yields cultural changing outcomes.

Historically, Behavior-Based Safety (BBS) has been a favored safety management practice within the fire service, based on my observations. BBS operates on the premise that humans can and should behave according to design for safe work execution. When deviations occur, human behaviors are often identified as the root cause or primary source of error. This approach, however, oversimplifies safety by reducing it to a mere behavioral issue. Humans make mistakes. However, organizational systems and environments are the predominant influences of human behavior.

Safety management must evolve beyond BBS to consider the broader operational contexts that influence human behavior. Deviations and drift will occur in any organization given enough time along with the need to get work done within operational time constraints. This doesn't mean discarding BBS entirely, but rather reconstructing operations to acknowledge that human behaviors are largely shaped by system design and environment.

Human Organizational Performance (HOP) is an operational philosophy grounded in the belief that processes, systems, environments, and experience are pivotal influences on human actions and choices. It recognizes that mistakes are an inherent part of being human. HOP principles redirect the focus of reviews away from individuals, understanding that errors and choices are primarily influenced by their surroundings. Adopting HOP principles fosters trust, prioritizes learning, and drives system improvements that enhance both reliability and resilience. Among its five principles, leadership's response is arguably the most critical for building initial trust and cultivating a learning environment.

Complex systems differ fundamentally from simple and complicated systems. Complexity arises from the varied and dynamic interactions of multiple interdependent systems. Internal and external relationships may be difficult to control and understand in real-time and will lack sufficient time to evaluate available decisions in emergency operations.

Simple systems involve linear cause-and-effect relationships that are easily identified and remedied. Complicated systems consist of components working together to perform a function, and their relationships are usually clearer before issues arise. In complex systems, known or unknown interdependencies can surprise human operators, and timing constraints hinder thorough analysis of operational decisions impacting safety and reliability. A significant strength of human operational performance lies in firefighters' inherent ability to adapt to system and environmental surprises.

The path for HSO/SOs involves discovering and pursuing work solutions that lead to higher reliability and enhanced resilience. Reliability signifies consistency in service delivery and practice. It also foreshadows resilience which can be described as the capacity or system flexibility to mitigate the consequences of failure. As the fire service's mission continually expands to meet evolving community needs, maintaining consistent service delivery becomes more challenging due to the constant evolution of delivery models and services. Reviewing both failed and successful operations should prioritize defining operational reliability before operations even commence, a process that demands considerable time from both management and labor.

Becoming a restorative practice organization represents one of the most impactful decisions an organization can make to improve learning and foster a sense of value among its members. When learning is enhanced and easily shared, safety and service delivery naturally improve because frontline workers are empowered to solve work-related problems and understand influential environmental factors. Seven specific practices can help an organization move towards a restorative approach, emphasizing that everyone shares responsibility for contributing to learning and problem-solving.

Managing bias is a critical component of organizational self-awareness and analysis, demanding significant reflection and constant vigilance in any review process. As humans, our emotional responses to our work are largely conditioned by our personal history and experience. Common biases encountered in reviews include confirmation bias and hindsight bias. To effectively manage bias, adhering to a structured analysis or sensemaking process is essential. Familiarity with common review process bias is also crucial.

Retributive practices severely impede learning by eroding trust and causing frontline workers to become unwilling to share information that might lead to punitive actions. Consequently, opportunities for improvement and learning are driven underground as workers revert to unchanged, "normal" conditions.

A leader's initial response after an event will be remembered. I propose that leadership's first step should be to reaffirm their commitment to learning. If words like "accountability" are prioritized, the opportunity for genuine learning may be lost, replaced by the belief that someone will be held solely responsible. While it's challenging to prioritize learning, if leadership (whether labor or management) doesn't take these initial steps, there is little hope of transitioning from retributive to restorative practices. It is crucial to avoid inadvertently creating "second victims."

Questions to Consider

1. Matching (one will not belong)
   Cultural artifacts _____
   Cultural values _____
   Cultural assumptions _____
a) Often unconscious, they come from life experiences and a desire to belong.
b) Language, procedures, organizational structure.
c) "The way we do things around here."
d) How we rationalize or justify behaviors; how realities are perceived.

2. T or F   We change culture by changing how we look, talk, and act.

3. T or F   Cultural influences compete with organizational priorities to negatively or positively impact our safety.

4. According to BBS, safer behaviors can be influenced through encouragement, _____, _____, and supervision.
a) Money, food
b) Fear, retribution
c) Blame, shaming
d) Training, education

5. T or F   Human error is normal and usually a combination of several organizational and human factors.

6. T or F   BBS investigations tend to highlight failure and risk, then seek top-down solutions.

7. HOP stands for:
a) Human operational performance
b) Hilarious organizational performances
c) Human organizational potential
d) Human organizational performance

8. T or F   HOP is an operational philosophy that believes individual behavior is influenced by processes, systems, environments, and experience.

9. Pick the most accurate HOP principle out of the three:
a) The type of work drives worker behavior.
b) The goal of HOP is to decide who did what.
c) Worker actions are driven by the context surrounding the event.

10. A good accident model to use for understanding complex systems is the:
a) Swiss cheese model
b) Domino model
c) Network of influence model
d) STAMP accident model

11. VUCA stands for:
a) Variability, uncertainty, complicated, ambiguity
b) Vicious, unhinged, chicken, attack
c) Volatility, uncertainty, complexity, ambiguity
d) Variability, uncertainty, simple, ambiguity

12. Which selection is considered a restorative practice for an organization?
a) Inclusive Committee Work
b) Make doing it right easy
c) Teach psychological safety
d) Manage language
e) All of the above
f) A, B, and C

13. T or F   Emotional conductivity is the process of emotions shaping an investigator's interpretation of evidence.

14. T or F   A review team facilitator naturally brings their past experiences, expectations, and emotional reactions that lead to theories or assumptions that become facts in the case.

15. Confirmation Bias is:
a) What we suffer from when we are looking to buy a new car.
b) How we prioritize information that confirms our good feelings that we bought a great new car.
c) Causes us to stress out when a senate confirmation hearing is commenced.
d) How we selectively tune out someone who is telling us to do something unpleasant.

16. Hindsight Bias is:
a) What an eye exam is called when our vision is 20/20.
b) Makes it difficult to understand why the decisions made were so poor.

c) It promotes tunnel vision when looking at an event through a participant's view.
d) None of the above.

17. Fundamental Attribution Error Bias:
a) Is my belief that the driver that cut me off is a better driver than me.
b) Is my belief that the chef who gave me a dry cut of steak has a personality that prevents him from understanding what medium rare is.
c) Is my belief that my friend got fired because he/she doesn't understand the fundamentals of business.
d) Prevents me from looking at the event I am reviewing because I can't fundamentally understand what was really going on.

18. T or F   One goal of a review is to understand the relationships between actions and context.

Section Three | Review Considerations

"The mark of a successful organization isn't whether or not it has problems, it's whether or not it has the same problems it had last year." – John Foster Dulles

Getting Started

Most people want to deliver responsible, fair and comprehensive findings about why an adverse event occurred. There is a common motivational belief that we will predict and prevent harmful events from recurring. This desire to prevent harm is healthy and understandable, and where possible, we should certainly strive to prevent injuries. However, it's important to remember that we simply cannot predict everything. The future remains uncertain. What we can do is help make operations more reliable under uncertain circumstances by increasing organizational resilience.

Humans operating within systems must contend with various factors: tools, time constraints, production pressures, safe work pressures, and more. When any of these relationships are under significant system pressure, we cannot be certain of the impact. As an example, when required regulatory training for maintaining certifications takes units out of service during high call volume periods. We hope those left to cover will manage the effects of higher call volumes and longer response times, but there are no guarantees. Due to system uncertainty, we find ourselves weighing the risks and benefits, embarking on less predictable futures with reduced capacities. If everything is managed successfully, a sense of optimism engendered by continued successes (section seven) might result. In a highly reliable organization this is cause for concern.

To truly understand how events influence frontline behaviors the fire service must develop its ability to make sense of and analyze events and then share those findings. Reviews offer a helpful framework for this. However, keep in mind this is not a purely technical pursuit. The first step in this process involves discerning which events warrant a review.

Minor Events

Minor events often arise from known hazards during familiar repetitive tasks, such as physical training injuries, apparatus striking objects in close quarters, or ankle sprains on uneven surfaces. While these usually don't necessitate full reviews, they do require curious discovery and assessment of how they transpired without fear of retribution for the reporting party. It can be particularly valuable to focus on minor to moderate event outcomes that are outliers, where a familiar and repetitive action yields an unexpected result.

Consider an apparatus operator performing a routine morning vehicle check, attempting to start a saw.

As the pull cord was tugged, it slipped, recoiling back forcefully and striking the operator's opposite hand on the middle finger, near the knuckle. Despite immediate swelling and soreness, the operator, wearing work gloves, shrugged it off and continued the check. Days later, persistent pain, swelling, and immobility prompted the operator to report the injury to the company officer. A visit to the occupational health provider revealed a bone fracture caused by the tool strike. The force was significant enough to push surrounding tissue into the fracture, leading to an infection that ultimately required surgery.

This unforeseen outcome of a routine inspection underscored the importance of the injury reporting program's directive: report all injuries, no matter how minor, without fear of reprisal. Without such compelling outlier stories (following a brief discovery and assessment) encouraging the reporting of all minor injuries can be challenging in any department.

This narrative was shared once the operator had recovered and sufficient time had passed to mitigate any embarrassment. It exemplifies how a familiar repetitive action with a surprising outcome can offer significant learning value and when such instances should be prioritized. In my experience with an organization comprising of hundreds of members, more immediate demands often prevented thorough attention to minor events, making it a continuous balancing act.

Assessing the Need for a Review

Nearly all adverse events warrant a brief verbal assessment to determine their learning value for the organization. Operationally, this means the department's SO or HSO should be notified of all accidents, injuries, and close calls as they occur, ideally within 24 hours or before the end of the shift. Supervisors of those reporting should be notified immediately to ensure reports are completed within established program timelines.

When filtering events for their learning potential the verbal assessment is crucial. Equally important is the assessor's (SO's/HSO's) demeanor. This individual should be approachable to all ranks and divisions within the fire department, possessing foundational characteristics such as humility and intelligence.

Assessments primarily focus on understanding what happened and providing the affected member an opportunity to recount their experience from their perspective. Conducting the assessment promptly is vital. Delays can lead to individuals filling in details with information from others or their own imagination, potentially distorting the actual experience. Memory is highly malleable as Borden notes, "Memory recall is subjective to biases, distortions, and limitations."[32] Therefore, gaining access to involved member experience, even if it seems disjointed, different, or unremarkable is invaluable. This immediate experience offers significant learning value, revealing what was understood during the event and highlighting the impact of factors like stress, fatigue, cognitive fixation or overload.

---

[32] Borden, Jamie. Critical Incident Review Blog, Referenced December 2024.

The initial assessment should be brief and concentrate solely on the event as it was experienced, along with preventing the narrative from straying. Exploration of other contextual factors such as organizational or personal cultural influences can be reserved for later, after the member has recounted their immediate memory of what actions they took. To keep things on task it helps to use the OODA loop in reverse.

We found that one-on-one interviews are generally more effective than group interviews for most events. Combining different ranks and experience levels in the same room can compromise psychological safety, recall accuracy, and divergent perspectives. Most event participants can be grouped together like a tree-ring model or metaphor for those involved. The inner ring (those who were closest to the incident) whether a single member or several, should be interviewed individually, while outer rings of activities may be reviewed together as teams.

Assessments serve as an initial information gathering step, leading to a decision about whether to proceed with a full review. It is critical to understand that reviews are neither retributive nor disciplinary HR processes. Should an HR process be required, it takes precedence, and reviews must either be postponed or foregone entirely. Never allow anyone to weaponize reviews by redirecting the intent to learn into a disciplinary procedure as this will severely undermine learning efforts and ultimately reduce overall safety.

A safety team I know had a chief officer who, in an emotionally charged moment, slammed a fist on the table, demanding to identify the individual responsible for an accident. It was an unconscious attempt to hijack the process, not a personal attack. The team courageously proceeded with their discovery work and sensemaking, producing a report that avoided blaming any single person. Fortunately, they heard no further demands from that chief after the report's completion. It likely helped that several decisions setting the stage for the accident had been made by chief officers, including the demanding officer.

While COVID-19 spurred the use of remote interviews, face-to-face remains the optimal method. Select a neutral location, free from distractions for both interviewer and interviewee. Be prepared to take notes and diagrams on paper and record the interview after obtaining permissions and signed nondisclosure agreements (NDAs). If a full review is warranted, the recorded assessment conversation should be transcribed for review and reference during the sensemaking and analysis phase.

Have a local legal representative draft a consent form that safeguards the confidentiality of the conversation and specifies its use solely for post-review purposes. Ensure both management and labor agree to this document, reinforcing that it is not an HR process. Both the interviewer and interviewee should sign the consent form before the assessment begins. Set time expectations that account for breaks and meals, especially for potentially lengthy assessments.

Any standard operating procedures (SOPs) outlining the assessment process should be general rather than overly specific, with an additional goal of protecting the affected member's identity. Maintain an informal and highly confidential assessment process. The core purpose of an initial assessment is to determine if a full review would be beneficial.

Almost every event possesses learning value. Decisions regarding the escalation of an assessment to a full review will also hinge on other factors, including the severity of the event (minor to severe), department size, available expertise, impact on public trust, and financial considerations. Organizational size may influence the formality of the review, the team resources available for conducting it, and budgetary constraints. Automatic aid agreements can also either assist or impede, particularly affecting a participant's candor when visiting an agency that experienced the consequences of an event. Be humble.

When to Conduct a Review

You can conduct a review anytime your organization wants to learn more about a process, make something more efficient, examine work that could be consequential, or ask your workforce what concerns them. Reviews are applicable to any work, process, or system.

However, repetitive events with familiar hazards and common controls may not hold as much learning potential as events with unfamiliar hazards that have difficult mitigation efforts and uncertain outcomes. When accidents, injuries, and close calls take place around unfamiliar hazards, unexpected energies, combinations of hazards that overtake system controls, or member training and experience, the potential for learning increases. Unexpected hazardous encounters or procedural deviations also equate to a high probability of learning. Knowing when an event crosses over into the category of offering a high degree of learning takes gained experience over time. Here is an example:

> Time of call: 14:20. Clear skies with temperatures in the high 90s. Crews were positioned on the freeway on-ramp at the tip (end) of the entry vortex for merging traffic onto the freeway. Two apparatus were positioned to restrict, but not completely block traffic, allowing traffic to move around them on the left. Cones were placed to regulate a left-side detour. Traffic could still merge onto the freeway, but around the scene. The intent was for traffic to gain access to the freeway by traveling left of the scene across or into the solid white line vortex with permission from DPS on the scene. The scene was against the right shoulder wall (elevated freeway) where left merge activity could take place with full view of oncoming freeway traffic which was passing by at full freeway speeds. The ambulance was downstream on the opposite end of the accident scene.
>
> A single vehicle attempting to merge was able to travel along the right shoulder wall past both parked apparatuses ending up inside the incident work zone without warning. Firefighters on the right shoulder wall had to jump up on the wall or car to escape injury. The driver was not impaired but was confused regarding travel lanes.

Unfortunately, cones were hurriedly placed to facilitate paramedic drivers getting up to the scene to help with patient care. Apparatus drivers who serve as paramedics needing to direct patient care dismounted the apparatus quickly and didn't check the barrier after placing cones. DPS had also made professionally polite statements at previous scenes about traffic control and how continued traffic flow was a huge need that came from their supervisors. One comment was, "The governor's office wants us to keep these roads open."

This close call demonstrates a familiar hazard that is repetitively encountered (traffic at MVA trauma medical calls) but experienced a rare outcome when a vehicle penetrated the safety barrier. Photos of the scene revealed shorter than recommended cone placements, smaller sized traffic cones not recommended for high-speed roadways, and apparatus placement which didn't provide the intended impenetrable barrier at an angle to the work zone. This close call yielded the following learning outcomes and operational challenges:

Findings
- On-ramps that travel up toward elevated roadways need longer distance cone placements than what procedures recommend, due to the terrain causing visibility restrictions.
- Apparatus cannot accommodate the taller, necessary cones due to limited cabinet space and height. Smaller cones are commonly being used by members to fit more cones in the apparatus cabinet. Over time, members have forgotten the importance of taller cones on high-speed roadways.
- In the past, apparatus placement on high-speed roadways has created goal conflict with DPS officers who have a gubernatorial mandate to keep freeways open. Apparatus drivers try to accommodate DPS needs and safe work zones, but at times leave penetrable barriers with the belief that as speeds naturally slow, the danger to all roadway workers lessens.
- Overall, more pronounced apparatus angles to protect the work zone are required, which will conflict with DPS's mission. DPS needs to be included in the conversation that would reexamine procedures for freeway operations.

NFPA Prompts for Conducting Reviews

Numerous formal documents set the standard for conducting reviews. Referencing NFPA standards is a good starting point. Below are applicable standards with paraphrased references.

NFPA 1021. Standard for Fire Officer Professional Qualifications, 2020
- 5.6.2 Develop and conduct a post-incident analysis, given a multi-unit incident and post-incident analysis policies, procedures, and forms, ensuring all required critical elements are identified and communicated, and approved forms are completed and processed.

- 5.7 The HSO has a duty to review injury, accident, and exposure reports with the goal of preventing future recurrences.
- 5.7.1 All relevant reports need to be considered, and recommendations made to supervisors.

NFPA 1550 Standard for Emergency Responder Health and Safety, 2024
   4.7 Accident Investigation, Procedures, and Review.
- This duty involves developing policies for and conducting accident and injury investigations, along with establishing procedures and coordinating actions to implement corrective actions.
- 4.7.1 Conduct a safety and health investigation, given an incident or planned event involving an occupational injury, illness, exposure, fatality, near miss, or other potentially hazardous conditions involving fire department members, fire department vehicles, apparatus, equipment or facilities, SOP/Gs, health and safety policies.
- 4.7.3 Establish procedures for a health and safety component of a post-incident analysis, given an incident or planned event, incident information, data, reports or records, SOP/Gs, necessary technical knowledge, and all applicable laws, regulations, and standards, so that risks to personnel are identified and reduced or eliminated at future incidents, and the applicable AHJ SOP/Gs are reviewed and revised as needed.
- 4.7.4 Coordinate the development of a corrective action plan, given a team, a list of recommendations arising from the investigation of occupational accidents, injuries, deaths, illnesses, exposures, observation of incident scene activities, and departmental policies and procedures, so that root causes are determined, the plan is documented, and controls are implemented according to departmental policies and procedures.

NFPA 1521. Standard for Fire Department Safety Officer Professional Qualifications, 2020.
   4.6 Accident Investigation, Procedures, and Review.
- 4.6.1 Conduct a safety and health investigation, given an incident or planned event involving an occupational injury, illness, exposure, fatality, near miss, or other potentially hazardous conditions, involving fire department members, fire department vehicles, apparatus, equipment or facilities, SOP/G's, health and safety policies, so that the facts and the root cause of the incident are correctly identified, deviations from SOP/G's established by the AHJ and health and safety policies are noted, recommendations are made for preventing similar losses in the future, and all information gathered in the investigation is documented, reported, and recorded according to policies established by the AHJ.
- 5.6.1 Conduct a safety and health investigative process, given an incident or planned event, using applicable documents and techniques, so that the chain of evidence is started and maintained, critical incident data elements are collected, potential witnesses are identified, applicable SOP/Gs are identified for review, and gathered information is documented and prepared for the HSO or investigative continuance as established by the AHJ policies and SOP/Gs.

I think it is helpful to use NFPA standards as part of your justification for conducting a review and delivering a report with an action plan. Copy and paste this verbiage into all your report introductions and your department's administrative policies. Make sure it makes sense for you and your organization, so it is transferable to the next generation of leaders.

Maintaining Confidentiality

For organizations that are struggling with trust between management and labor or moving away from retributive practices to restorative practices, analyzing close calls may be one of the most beneficial ways to build trust. Some good advice I found early on was to avoid blaming any single member or group of members and keep all identities confidential by scrubbing the call of identifiers that would reveal locations or units operating on the incident at the time of the event. Controlling the identities helps to reduce any related embarrassment or bravado. Neither is helpful for the acceptance of review outcomes. Remember, we are not interested in who, but rather in the why and how.

I understand it is extremely difficult to maintain confidentiality because members involved will talk especially, and quite naturally, because some events are high-profile. It is still essential for the long-term effort toward building trust that the review team is not doing any of the talking. Review team members should all sign NDAs. Trust is built by respecting the privacy of members who come forward to share information. Reviews should become historical records for your department. Omitting the identifiers helps to maintain the professional appeal of the review for future training division use.

Making Complexity Transparent

Reviews illuminate hidden or weak signal vulnerabilities and seek to make complex organizational relationships evident. Once we learn to listen and analyze operations without judgment, we can build trust and perhaps discover unknown problems. The following story illustrates how complex relationships can become dangerous when not fully vetted for the impact they will have on all operations. As departments try to make their operations more proficient, some actions can cause reactions that may not have been considered.

Interagency operations are beneficial to communities because they save money and bolster capacity for participating agencies. Common to fire districts — their coverage areas may include two or three law enforcement (LE) agencies. Fire municipalities often operate with one police department from the same city or county. Fire departments commonly learn to communicate with the LE agencies within their jurisdictions.

> A residential fire started in an area covered by a fire district. The fire district requested mutual aid from a municipal fire department. A new policy existed that stipulated if the two agencies worked together, they would use the dispatch center and radio channel of the municipality. It had more capacity, offered redundancy, and had a single designated alarm room dispatcher. Upon arrival of the municipal department, everyone switched channels as the residential firefight was already underway.

Once communication moved from the district's fire channel to the municipal fire channel, communications with the county LE agency were lost because the municipal fire agency did not share preset fire radio channels with the county LE. Two things were noticed by a Command Team Safety Officer. First, they weren't gaining access to the interior of the residence due to blocked doors and windows. Second, three different law enforcement agencies were on the scene, including the highway patrol (they were never on these local fire scenes), and all the officers were carrying semi-automatic rifles, and they seemed rather frantic.

One of the LE officers was stopped and asked by the Safety Officer, "Why the long guns?" The officer replied, "The homeowner is up on a knoll behind the house with a rifle. We think he wants to shoot first responders."

Findings: (not complete)
- Communication between the law enforcement agencies within the initial jurisdiction and their communication center were good.
- Communication between the fire agencies and their communications center were good.
- Redundant fire command team officers added extra eyes and ears (capacity) on the scene, and the elevated police activity was noticed.
- LE officers noticed firefighters were still trying to fight the fire, which seemed rather heroic to them, given the threat. However, it didn't cause them to pause and check to see if communication was missed. It was assumed to be "normal."
- Firefighters were frustrated at the lack of access and were readying bigger, more destructive tools to get inside. The barricading didn't register as abnormal; it was an issue that needed to be overcome.
- An alert dispatcher in the fire dispatch center noticed something was odd and made phone calls to all the LE agencies involved, trying to figure out what was all the noise on the LE "hot" channels about? In total, the dispatcher made 14 calls between three LE agencies before being able to piece together the threat to fire personnel.
- The on-scene Safety Officer called a full stop to operations and had everyone take cover behind buildings and began telling bystanders to take cover as well.
- County LE did not have the ability to reach Fire Command by radio, nor did they make the time, as these first-in LE officers had plenty to do "circling the wagons" and readying an attack up the knoll.
- The homeowner made a 911 call announcing his intentions. This information was taken in by the LE Public Safety Answering Point (PSAP) but didn't get passed to fire dispatchers in other PSAPs.
- The scene responsibility of informing the firefighters got lost in the initial scramble because it wasn't noticed until they needed to use the municipal fire radio channel that the county and state LEs didn't have.

Sharing the findings with LE in a nonconfrontational manner is usually well received. What I've noticed with LE agencies is that their missions are just as broad as ours, maybe even more so. Have patience when identifying LE officers who want to work well with fire and seek their input.

The complexity and tight coupling of this event is evident. Prior historical decisions had an adverse effect on operations. Weak signals at prior events (major medicals with poor communication, water rescues that lacked coordination, and wildland fires without LE accountability) were missed. However, this review captured the complexities and had an action plan that moved all the organizations toward greater capacity for future operations.

Surveying How Work Is Done

Reviews should encompass all types of operational events—failures, successes, accidents, injuries, and especially close calls. Every division within a fire department experiences incidents equally deserving of consideration. The examples below illustrate events that if they were only close calls without significant damage or injury, might have gone unnoticed and unassessed depending on the organization's reporting culture.

- An overpressure nut fails, and the sound emitted injures hearing.
- Dispatch software freezes up at 2100 hrs. on a Friday night, disrupting call dispatching for over four hours.
- The floor jack in the shop, used to lift a pickup truck for a tire change, had a hydraulic failure. The mechanic jumped out of the way, but the parts cleaner was knocked over, spilling its contents.
- A prevention officer, stopping to help a stranded motorist, had their unmarked sedan struck from behind as they pulled over to the right shoulder. No one was injured.
- A prevention officer was inspecting a CO_2 fire suppression system when it was accidentally triggered, forcing workers to evacuate. The workers made it out safely.

SO/HSOs must cultivate relationships with all departmental personnel, otherwise crucial weak signals will be overlooked. When events like those above are dismissed as mere operational mishaps significant learning opportunities are lost. For SO/HSOs, being present, engaging in casual conversations, and clearly communicating the safety mission are essential to understanding and supporting the safety of all department members.

It is vital to recognize how various pressures impact firefighters' work. These include internal personnel pressures related to staffing, as well as personal pressures concerning mental and physical wellness. Organizational morale issues also influence the willingness to share daily work struggles. External political pressures from outside agencies or groups can affect fiscal well-being, regulations, employment laws, environmental laws, taxation, media attention, and bureaucratic demands. These diverse pressures are experienced differently and are constantly negotiated by our workforce, yet our members consistently find ways to remain efficient. Missing these work performance changes and adaptations means missing key insights. Therefore, SOs/HSOs must regularly engage with personnel at the sites where the work is performed.

Actively seek instances where "work as imagined" (procedures and policies) subtly or vastly differs from "work as performed." If you observe closely, you will find that policies and procedures are rarely executed exactly as written or trained. Often, highly competent workers are adapting to unexpected, unplanned, or inefficient nuances of their tasks. In most cases, these adaptations lead to successful outcomes. Reviews must capture these successes, especially when work deviates from standard procedures. This understanding may reveal opportunities to eliminate or rewrite outdated procedures. By understanding how your members respond and think, you can identify and address operational gaps that compromise their ability to adapt when unforeseen circumstances arise.

Is Root Cause Helpful?

If you've ever investigated, you've probably experienced the pressure to find a root cause. Root cause is the belief that every accident has a primary trigger or reason that will reveal the main cause for the event. If it could have been caught, noticed, or altered prior to the event, everything could have been prevented, resulting in a less destructive outcome. The belief that a root cause can always be determined is robust. If we drill down a bit deeper, we'll discover this belief is rooted in another belief or desire that everything can be prevented. I have learned that finding a root cause may feel like a worthy cause, but a root cause rarely exists when humans are operating within complex systems.

First, let's look at where root cause analysis may work well. If reviewing a simple cause-and-effect failure, it tends to work, but the investigator should be trained on how easy it is to fall prey to bias and miss actual root causes altogether. To illustrate what is simple, I remember reading a close call report about a firefighter starting a circular saw during a morning check. The blade spun off the saw, then rolled some distance away, crossed a street, struck the cement curb, and came to rest. Determining the root cause involved identifying either a) the previous shift not tightening the blade, or b) a failure to check the blade tightening nut prior to the morning check. This adverse event had a simple cause-and-effect relationship. If a blade spins fast enough and it isn't tightened sufficiently, centrifugal force will not be adequately contained by the tool. Simple inspection of the tool will rule out stripped threads as a contributing factor. Regardless, this is a linear cause-and-effect event situation: if blade tightening nuts are not tightened, the blade can come off.

Where root cause analysis does not work well is when complexity enters the equation. Remember, complexity occurs when several parts or several systems interact with conflicting goals and pressures simultaneously in real time. Firefighters, often acting under time constraints and duress, make decisions within multifaceted contexts including relationships between people, processes, technology, and machines, then strive to create the best outcomes they can. Failure under these circumstances isn't linear cause-and-effect, like the linear failure of an untightened blade falling off a saw. Learning from complex events requires broader consideration of causation as multifaceted.

Narrative

At approximately 0432, an Engine Company struck an awning in a private business parking lot near a local hospital while attempting to turn around to take a shorter route to quarters. This incident was an accident and a close call due to the major intrusion of the awning's fascia aluminum trim penetrating the driver's windshield well into the driver's space. Once the apparatus came to a stop, the crew found one of the two intrusion pieces stopped approximately 6 inches from the driver's face, while the other passed by the driver's head on the right and traveled three feet into the rear cabin area. There were no injuries.

Findings in a narrative format:

After conducting a review, multiple influential factors for this close call were identified. Members who possess a "can-do" work ethic, working under the pressures of limited training opportunities and increased call volume demands, normalized procedurally deviant behaviors in the belief their actions were aligned with other legitimate organizational goals. Past success and approval while conducting these actions also led them to believe their behaviors were sanctioned by management. Operationally, crews incrementally deviated from procedures and believed they were encouraged to continue. Results indicate company officer training may have  insufficiencies regarding intentional supervision of members who have "moved up" or shifted into roles they normally do not perform.

The driver's mindset in this event as an Acting Engineer (driver) was limited due to fatigue (third call after 2200), a concern for an (8) hour day of upcoming paramedic training the following day after a sleep-deprived night of calls, and personal pressures related to his/her contractual closing on the purchase of a new home. The driver's experience was limited due to insufficient opportunity to drive because of competing paramedic training, which reduced shift time for driving, and having no night driving experience.

The driver's vision was also limited due to internal cab reflected lighting. First, reflected light on the windshield originated from an open MDT monitor between the driver and company officer. Second, extremely bright external flood lighting 150 feet behind and beyond the awning severely obscured vision of the awning itself.

Finally, the driver was avoiding a ground-level curb on the rear right side, visible through the right-side review mirror, which influenced the decision to take the turn wide to the left, striking the awning. None of the crew were assisting with the driving task. The acting captain was entering data into the dash-mounted mobile data terminal; the actual crew captain, in the right rear jump seat, was filling out an EMS form on a portable tablet; and the other firefighter in the left jump seat was talking to the captain.

An emphasis on finding a root cause and blaming the driver would miss broader opportunities to learn from the context that reveals deeper issues at play here. The broader system issues of supervision and competing needs (offering drive time for task books and training paramedics on their day off to save costs) along with the individual issues of cognitive fixation, fatigue, and lighting, all factor into the context that influenced decisions leading up to the event.

Other factors of procedural deviation (drift), and a culture of asking new members to contribute beyond their comfort level (psychological safety) were discussed later in the report but are not included here. Root cause analysis in this situation would not have challenged the systems that set the stage for goal conflicts and pressures to perform under varying circumstances. We learn much more from conducting reviews designed to uncover the broad factors that influenced behaviors allowing for alterations to prevent future catastrophic events.

Organizations commonly ask, what was the root cause and what can be done to prevent this in the future? The feeling of getting to the bottom of a situation is legitimized in society, but I'm not sure it's helping us learn how to transform our organizations. Instead, we settle for transactions that essentially say, "Ok, you screwed up, now pay through some form of social, psychological, or punitive measure." Failure commonly becomes transactional instead of what we need it to be, transformational. I hope you can feel this difference.

The desire to find root cause and the person who failed is rooted in old, tired beliefs that our problems are easily correctable because they seem relatively small. We don't see the need to continually renew or remodel operations. The truth is your operations are continually degrading one way or another. Equipment gets old, outdated procedures are skipped or ignored, expectations change becoming harder to reach, and as money gets tight, staffing adjusts. Whatever the situation your ops are not the same as they were just a few months ago. Degradation takes place incrementally, slowly, without notice.

The pursuit of root cause in more serious events results in anemic reports about what happened, not why it happened. We want to believe cause is linear, that it is simple to determine if we ask enough why questions. So, when human error becomes the root cause, and it commonly appears to be, narrative findings include statements like "FF wasn't aware," "mechanic failed to follow procedure," "company officer was complacent," "trainee was unfamiliar with the limitations of the tool." The list goes on, but what's happening is that the training, the time commitment, and the bias of the reviewer ends up calling a stop to the deeper search for context and settles for things that are easily correctable. A shallow review is usually a result of an untrained, inexperienced investigator. I suggest you steer away from the idea that a root cause exists for fire service accidents or any other adverse, unexpected outcome. Rarely, and I mean rarely, will adverse events be linear and have a single root cause. We are complex organizations dealing with complex problems in uncertain, ambiguous environments. Influences come from all directions.

Section Three Summation

Not every adverse event needs to be fully reviewed, but it can be difficult to sift and filter which events should or shouldn't be reviewed. When managing minor events sift for outlier outcomes that offer support for your program goals. Also, record and watch for data that offers direction or feedback to your program objectives or changes. Conducting assessments is best done in person, within a day or two of the events. The sooner the better.

When a routine repetitive event has an unexpected outcome, or a successful event has elements of failure that were overcome, reviews should be conducted to consider as much context surrounding the event as possible. This will help to make transparent why or how decisions were made which resulted in the outcome(s).

NFPA has several standards that encourage retrospectively looking at operations. They all reiterate the need to investigate how failure occurred. Conducting a review meets NFPA's standards and should also take control of maintaining confidentiality to build trust and expose complexity so members can learn about what's going on around them. It also helps the SO/HSO understand what or how work is getting done in the field. You can conduct a review anytime your organization wants to learn more about a process, make something more efficient, look at work that could be consequential, or ask your workforce what's concerning to them. Reviews are applicable to any work, process, or system.

Reviews can flush out hidden or weak signal vulnerabilities and should seek to make complex organizational relationships transparent. Unfortunately, it is likely we will not find all the weak signals in our organizations with just a single review. The culturally influenced behaviors that reviews identify will help to enable our firefighters see system interdependencies as systems become more complex and interrelated.

All divisions within a fire department have events that are equally deserving of review consideration. Both successful operations and failed operations have educational benefit. It is most important that SO/HSOs get out of the office and talk to firefighters and staff to determine what types of events are happening, especially the events that did not result in an adverse outcome.

Root cause should be used judiciously on linear cause-and-effect types of events. Using root cause on complex events where humans are interacting within systems reduces learning and may result in using corrective actions to fix firefighters who may have made a mistake. Resist the prompts and closed-door meetings that push for a root cause. It just isn't useful for a complex adverse event.

Questions to Consider

1. T or F   Accidents are predictable.

2. Minor events usually result from:
a) Known hazards while conducting familiar, repetitive actions.
b) Unknown hazards while conducting familiar, repetitive actions.
c) Known hazards while conducting familiar, nonrepetitive actions.
d) Unknown hazards while conducting familiar, nonrepetitive actions.

3. For most adverse event reviews:
a) A total of four reviewers is necessary. Two to be on standby.
b) Two reviewers are necessary. One to lead and the other to assist.
c) Two review facilitators are best. One with knowledge of the event.
d) Associates of the people involved in the event are the best facilitators of a review.

4. Serious event reviews result from:
a) Events with unfamiliar hazards.
b) Events with difficult mitigation efforts.
c) Events that had familiar hazards that experienced a rare outcome.
d) All the above.
e) None of the above.

5. NFPA prompts for conducting investigations/reviews through the following standards:
a) 1021-Standard for Fire Officer Professional Qualifications
b) 1550-Standard on Fire Department Occupational Safety, Health, and Wellness Program
c) 1091-Standard on Fire Department Incident Safety Officer Professional Qualifications
d) A and B only.

6. Root Cause investigative methodology is helpful when looking into:
a) A close call at a residential fire with a roof collapse.
b) An apparatus accident with heavy damage to a nursing home driveway cover.
c) The failure of a floor jack in the shop.
d) The injury of a fire recruit during a live training event.

7. T or F   A SO/HSO should regularly visit firefighters and staff in their stations and offices.

Section Four | Discovery of Information

The three phases of the review process are discovering information, sensemaking/analysis, and sharing findings. The idea here is to conduct your discovery and sensemaking of the event within a framework, then extract and interpret what constitutes valuable learning for your organization. Remember however, what is valued by your organization may not be valued as much by another. So don't look for similar types of findings given similar operational circumstances elsewhere.

Discovering information involves collecting as much information and data about the event as possible. Helpful programs like the National Safety Council's Incident Investigation Virtual One Day Course (8 hours), or OSHA's 7505 Introduction to Incident (Accident) Investigation (15 hours) are introductory classes that familiarize attendees with basic data gathering skills. If you take these classes, watch out for language that signals root cause as the overall outcome of investigative findings. Because these courses are introductory, failure or error can be oversimplified to keep the class on an easy-to-follow trajectory. Gathering data for more serious, nonlinear, complex incidents usually requires greater effort in the interview process.

There are more sophisticated books and software-based programs for identifying root cause that I have attended but choose not to name here. These are general industry programs that are not fire service specific, and by using their decision trees or software, users can search for root cause phrases and corrective actions. There has always been quite an appetite for root cause across all industries. Some programs admit there can be several root causes, which I think really starts to confuse the issue. In my experience, except for simple cause-and-effect types of events (i.e., tool breaks, machine failures, slips, trips, and most falls), root cause will not help your organization learn much about the deeper cultural assumptions that influence the "why and how" of events.

We live in litigious times. Therefore, internal reviews must take a back seat to criminal and civil litigation. There isn't much we can do about it except wait our turn. You may have access to information but not be allowed to act upon it organizationally. From state to state, attorney to attorney, determine how much action you can take. Remember to use your chain of command before talking to an attorney.

Collecting Equipment

When I was called out to adverse events, I found it most helpful to consult an experienced fire investigator for advice on how to gather evidence properly. The OSHA 7505 class teaches this, but I had some good investigators I could lean on for help, not just in my own agency, but in neighboring agencies as well. Be sure to exchange contact information with an experienced investigator. I was never turned down when I asked for help bagging and tagging equipment that needed closer inspection or needed to be photographed at the scene, or later in a less emotional setting when we needed more detail. Investigators can expertly organize and photograph the scene and will work closely with you on what pictures will be most helpful. If you work with law enforcement (LE) technicians it may require some approvals to smooth out the use of LE personnel and equipment, especially for photography. Often, LE must account for every photo taken with a camera.

There are proper ways to collect equipment involved in an event especially if it should be sent to a certified lab, technician, or the manufacturer for a detailed report about its condition. Use latex gloves, brown paper bags, and larger cardboard boxes when removing larger items like SCBAs. Avoid unnecessary handling. The larger the group involved in the event, the larger the room you will need to lay out all the equipment for tagging and reference. Tag along with a fire investigator and watch how they bag, tag, and categorize items.

Help with turnouts can be referred through your cleaning vendor or turnout care contractor. As the contract comes up for renewal make sure to add in features that include helping with unexpected events involving turnouts if you haven't already. Also, ensure your SCBAs can be inspected by the vendor caring for them or ensure the person internally managing their care is certified to do so and knows how to handle SCBAs involved in adverse events. Most technical equipment can be sent back to the manufacturer because they have considerable experience analyzing and sending a report about equipment condition. Just make sure you thoroughly photograph anything you send out. The photos will prove invaluable for illustrative purposes and for future identification of potential problems. Fire investigators and LE technicians know which local labs can provide scientific services that might help with your reports. Lab reports add credibility, which is valuable for your report.

The same goes for apparatus. LE accident scene technicians or detectives will help with gathering the needed or applicable data. If things are not criminal or moving toward civil litigation you should be able to gather the data for your sensemaking/analysis phase.

Collecting Witness Accounts

Over the years, we tried several different ways to interview members involved in events. As I mentioned earlier, we found one-on-one, face-to-face interviews to be the best, especially for the "inner ring" of members involved. Context closest to the event usually has good operational value, so the need to capture it in its purest form is why one-on-one works best. If others are present (perhaps an overbearing company officer, or an over-opinionated firefighter), they can influence what gets spoken and we want to avoid that. Quiet, distraction-free, comfortable table and chair spaces are required. Use an audio recording device with proper agreements in place. Remember, this is going to be a deep dive into the spectrum of influence and information so be warm, patient, reassuring, and nonjudgmental.

Essentially, the first goal is to ask members about what they remember through their senses of sight, sound, smell, taste (if applicable), and touch. Often, much of this information will come out on its own, you just need to be patient and coax it out. In the beginning, it is not as important to hear chronological accounts as much as it is to draw out what they can recall from raw memory. If you are available enough to conduct an interview immediately post-event (give members a chance to rehab and get cleaned up) don't be surprised if the member is still sensemaking as they verbalize the event. This is natural and necessary for psychological health, but the story may sound jumbled or go back and forth. Also, don't be surprised if you begin to wonder if some of your witnesses were even on the same call together! What they saw and heard can be night and day from one member to the next. Keep listening and taking notes. Don't judge.

After sufficient time to recall what happened has been made in an interview it is helpful to ask what worked well and what didn't work well. What do they remember thinking while the event was in motion? Can they remember a time when something similar happened, or they had done it the same way, but the outcome was different? What motivated them to take the actions (or inactions) they did? What was odd or different, helpful, or unhelpful in terms of procedures, communication log jams, and whether past training was helpful for this event. This line of questioning, outside of raw event recall, helps uncover learning areas. As mentioned earlier, good framework to use is the OODA loop in reverse to gain insight into what actions were taken, what decisions led to the actions, what was their orientation, and what was observed.

If your event has citizen witnesses, especially citizen video, do your best to collect it in a central department repository. A department PIO may already have a link for video data to be uploaded and collected.

After I read Sidney Dekker's *The Field Guide to Understanding Human Factors*,[33] I started working on a fire service-specific model for conducting reviews. *The Field Guide to Understanding Human Factors* is a must-read book. Not only does it contain information about the factors listed below, but it sets the stage for everyone's understanding of error context. I commonly recall Dekker's phrase, "Get in the tunnel with them," and I repeat it in my mind during interviews. Getting into the tunnel is important

---

[33] *The Field Guide to Understanding Human Error,* S. Dekker, Ashgate Publishing Limited. Surrey England. 2006.

because we mentally place ourselves in the event, instead of the advantageous position of knowing the outcome and all the relevant factors. Being in the tunnel is about understanding how limited the information was at the time. This is why I recommend one interviewer not know the details of the event. It is easier to get in the tunnel when we don't know a lot about what happened.

As your interview skills grow you will discover language and identify behaviors that describe the following physical, mental and emotional factors. You will learn to probe without being pushy, overly focused on details and quickly catch words or phrases that connect to these common factors. Listen and probe into the following:

- Cognitive fixation or overload.
- Sticking to the original plan no matter what.
- Distress that slows thought or comprehension.
- Fatigue.
- Erroneous or inaccessible knowledge.
- New or unfamiliar equipment.
- Procedural over-adherence, under-adherence, and "on-the-fly" adaptations.
- Inability to recover or stabilize the event.
- Expected and unexpected results from responder's actions.
- Conflicting goals between production, efficiency, and safety.
- What seemed normal and what seemed abnormal.
- Familiar or previous experience that didn't apply this time to this event.
- Outside or learned behaviors that influenced actions.

These areas need to be probed and opened as completely as possible. This form of interviewing (cognitive) is more about completeness versus accuracy. We are probing for the depth of influences that may become part of our network of influences map (See *Guide to Performing a Review*). Make short notes of what is being revealed in the interview so you can use the notes after all the interviews are done.

Building Narratives

Developing a detailed narrative is meant to not only capture what happened, but why it happened. After consolidating all the interviews and reconciling them with the audio and video data, the initial narrative can be developed. This initial narrative should be a brief explanation of what happened that is completed within the first 48-96 hours and is often called a green sheet or a tactical incident review sheet (Phoenix/Mesa Regional Response System). Green sheets provide a very brief explanation of an event without going into any detail about why the event may have taken place. The purpose here is to inform the organization what happened, the condition of anyone injured, and generally set the stage for the next level of narrative. The green sheet may include one diagram and perhaps one photo. It shifts the review's focus from who was involved to how and why the event took place.

As the review process moves into the next phase a more detailed narrative of the actions taken that preceded the event should contain diagrams, photographs, edited video, interview transcripts, applicable policies, test results of equipment involved, and any other items important to the peer team selected to conduct the sensemaking analysis phase. If a map of influences was developed, that should be included as well.

Photos, video, and audio recordings are helpful for establishing minutes and seconds of any timeline, if you use one. It's very helpful to acquire stationary command vehicle video with the audio in the background throughout the event. However, not all incident commanders have the audio portion turned on for obvious, colorful reasons.

Section Four Summation

The information discovery phase consists of properly collecting equipment and data, gathering witness accounts, and then building an initial timeline to help describe the event. Asking for help from fire investigators and law enforcement scene technicians when collecting equipment, recording accident scene data, or photographing evidence is helpful and maintains a professional effort.

Interviewing members involved in an adverse event is delicate. Initially, the goal is to see what each person remembers in their own words without any help or judgment. To do this, the interview should take place as soon as practical after the event. Firefighters/staff being interviewed should <u>not</u> have access to video or audio data and should try not to talk to anyone else involved until they can be interviewed. Do not be surprised if their account of the events sounds disjointed.

A goal for the interviewer is to "get into the tunnel" with the person recalling the event.

Questions to Consider

1. There are three phases to conducting a review. They are:
a) Discover, Discernment, Decision
b) Discover, Sensemaking, Legal
c) Discover, Legal Evaluation, Decision
d) Discover, Sensemaking, Share Findings

2. T or F   It is a good idea to ask for fire investigators or law enforcement scene technicians to help you collect, bag and tag, and organize items collected at an adverse event.

3. T or F   You should expect participants at an adverse event to remember the chronological order of the event.

4. T or F   Green sheets describe a brief explanation of the event and should be done within 96 hours of an event.

Section Five | Sensemaking and Analysis

"We thought we had the answers, it was the questions we had wrong." – Bono

Sensemaking and analysis initially seems like a daunting task. Just the term analysis is a bit scary and sounds official. A Merriam-Webster definition of analysis states, "a detailed examination of anything complex in order to understand its nature or to determine its essential features."[34] When hunting to learn from events, detailed examinations will take time to understand. The work is making sense of how or why things happened and what the essential learning points will be for your organization. I personally have found this phase to be the most rewarding. Watching peers bring their understanding of how things work and why, then trying to understand someone else's behavior is challenging and the team always seems to like the challenge. Some say it made them reconsider why they do what they do since they never really thought about it.

One advantage we have in the fire service when conducting reviews is we tend to have enough peers who have similar training and experience in firefighting, emergency medical care, haz mat, TRT, driving, and pumping apparatus. If your organization is small, you might struggle when a mechanic gets injured, and you only have two. Or a dispatcher makes a mistake and it's the county sheriff that does your dispatching. It may take some time to find a peer group that can analyze an event for pertinent findings, but it is a necessary component of a review. What we want to avoid is anything that looks like a top-down analysis of higher-ranking officers evaluating the frontline, pointing out mistakes.

The longer-term effort of building controls to make work easy to do safely and hard to do unsafely is a big reason for using peer analyzers to create workable solutions that they can use. Again, this avoids the common mistake of falling back into the cycle of having management look at errors, then design a solution, only to discover later it didn't work or have any usefulness. Using peers to conduct the analysis breaks the cycle of management innocently or purposefully controlling which investigative findings have meaning, versus those doing the work who understand conflicting work priorities.

Most fire departments have spent time since 2011 learning how modern fire versus legacy fires should be managed differently. Hopefully everyone took advantage of the research and training. The research was clear. Expect early heat acceleration, accumulation of dense smoke, early flame reduction due to low O2 levels in a closed container, then rapid fire growth with the addition of fresh air.

Now, let's assume your department had a close call after your modern vs. legacy training. The close call review revealed tactics for legacy firefighting were present everywhere. No one noted the flow of the smoke upon entry. No one timed the ventilation. No one did a 360 to find an alternative exterior attack location. No one closed doors as they advanced through the structure, and windows were broken on two sides to gain access. A crew on the second floor ends up being overcome by sudden

---

[34] https://www.merriam-webster.com.

heat and was forced to take refuge in a bedroom to escape through the window once a ladder was raised.

First, acknowledge this event from a management perspective knowing possibly tens of thousands of dollars were spent training crews for new operations at this type of a fire. It was their belief that this training and education would change firefighting behaviors. From management's perspective it all makes sense, and it is safer to conduct operations this way.

Their response would be to question the officers in charge to find out why actions were void of modern fire behavior firefighting tactics. But remember the fifth HOP principle, "leadership's response matters." So hopefully they will contain their disappointment for enough time to ask a peer team to make sense out of this close call for everyone involved.

Now, examine the limited information offered here and consider facilitating a review by peers that will question why the firefighting decisions seemed right to them at the time. You might get a different understanding for why they did what they did and how they came to those decisions. If your peer team digs deep enough, they may find the education and training didn't offer task training of crews, coordination and communication practice with other crews, and changes to tactical worksheets. Hose line choices on trucks were still set to support quick attack legacy fires, and everyone on the scene still has a basic assumption that if you're not moving and getting something done, you're lazy, incompetent, or complacent. All of this is influential context. And who better to analyze this than their peers? And, who better to explain how decisions were made and why, than their peers who experience similar circumstances?

Peers will be able to outline how the organization will embrace the modern fire behavior tactics in the future. Allow peers to increase hose diameters on apparatus, eliminating poor hose choices, change nozzle types, develop procedures on when 360 and smoke condition reports will be given, and how to look for exterior locations to anchor the fire attack prior to any interior fire operations. Let peers decide how to best encourage, enforce, and audit fire attack operations, because they are the best ones to determine how to make good decisions easy and poor decisions hard.

When attempting to analyze and make sense out of an event context it is helpful to consider influential factors commonly found in adverse events across a broad base of industries. The list below is not in any order, but it will offer the peer team a framework to consider when sensemaking and analyzing various event factors. It is by no means all-inclusive or necessary to use the whole list on every review.

Some Common Factors to Consider

Cognitive Fixation or Overload

When members lose the ability to objectively consider themselves in relation to what surrounds them, they begin to lose the ability to make good decisions because information is no longer being processed thoughtfully. Cognitive overload manifests into an inability to process thought that would bring deeper awareness of the situation, but it is not situational awareness per se.

When environmental factors overload our senses, or a small but meaningful element of a chaotic scene distracts attention, or a fast-moving situation that has never been seen before is encountered, cognitive processes can get overloaded. Cognition can become fixated on incomplete or irrelevant data that is not broken down into smaller segments to manage the information. This leads to decision-making that looks poor in hindsight.

The goal of sensemaking and analysis is to understand why the member's cognitive understanding at the time made sense to them. If their actions changed during the event, why did they change? Or if they did not change when they should have, a facilitated peer analysis process seeks to understand how much data overloaded or captured their cognition at the time.

Essentially, was the person making decisions given adequate opportunity (as judged by peers) to understand what the situation encompassed? Peers should seek to understand what assessments were made and was information adequately ordered or prioritized. If cognitive fixation or overload interfered with decisions, how did that look, and can a logical assumption be offered to confirm the presence of cognitive fixation/overload? Can future operators be trained to recognize and counter fixation and overload?

Sticking to The Plan No Matter What

Plans and circumstances at emergencies change. Risk/benefit analysis should be conducted routinely (several times or at specific benchmarks) at events to ensure firefighters are not subjected to inappropriate risks. Although sticking to the plan is a close relative to cognitive fixation, it has more to do with the ongoing decision-making, or the lack thereof. When situation parameters change, the original plan is not altered or stopped. In fact, sometimes the original plan will get a doubling down effort.

Peers should look for overly ambitious or under resourced initial plans that make it less likely for members to catch obvious, subtle, or gradual changes. Peers should analyze to understand why sticking to the plan made sense at the time. What factors did people close to the event rely on that made the continuation of the plan appropriate? If a plan change had a cost, what was it? Peers need to determine what dynamics related to keeping the plan in place were considered.

Distress

In the realm of stress there is good and bad stress. Good stress, eustress, quickens our pulse and excites us without any threat or fear. Eustress motivates and inspires us. Bad stress, meaning too much stress or distress, leads to anxiety and eventually to poorer performance. When we are confused under a time constraint, or face a life-altering threat, it is inevitable our cognitive concentration will diminish, rendering decision-making difficult.

Events, especially at onset, can quickly become a mismatch between situational demands and the resources that need to be mustered to manage mitigation. Our sense of time will be distorted as higher workloads competing for our attention cause distress leaving less mental ability to track time. Peer teams should listen for a sense of lost time or look for how time keeping became misinterpreted. This is why fire ground timers are so important.

Peer analysis should also look for other personal or social factors causing stress that may impact thoughts and decisions. Often stressful personal, relational, and financial issues follow members into work, adding distress to everyday work decisions and attention. Acute distress of any kind can result in reduced ability to see the whole operational environment and favor the use of previously learned routines that may not be applicable to the event at hand.

Fatigue

Fatigue slows and clouds decisions and judgment. At one time or another most departments will decide about shift work schedules. As they do, everyone scrambles for shift-work related fatigue studies that support their position. What I found in my research several years ago was a lack of quantitative research that considered the 24 or 48-hour shifts with variable call volumes, and/or variable sleep cycles. Most shift studies were for 8 to 12-hour shifts, and night shifts that interfered with the circadian sleep cycles.

Analysis of fatigue seeks information about performance impairment that can be related to an immediate previous history of poor-quality sleep. Analysis should also look at workload and exertion prior to the event. Fatigue interferes with attention span, it slows reasoning, makes memory recall less efficient, and can result in firefighters zoning out, even interfering with the ability to physically do the work.

Erroneous or Inactive Knowledge

Fire needs to have air, fuel, and heat. Remove one element and the fire goes out. We all know this. Knowledge of fire triangles and tetrahedrons similarly needs to be available (mentally) so it can be usable at an event. What peer analysis looks for under this factor is, did those involved have knowledge of the factors involved and were they able to access and use the knowledge in a timely manner?

Correct or incorrect information is usually a function of training both at an academy or some form of OJT. Some training is highly controlled while other types are not. It is usually the uncontrolled OJT that brings erroneous knowledge to a crew or can grow like a virus among groups as large as a whole shift. As peer analysis is conducted erroneous knowledge will be discovered from time to time. The analysis effort should document its presence and turn that information over to the training division in a nonjudgmental, confidential manner.

Peer teams should consider determining if the correct knowledge was on the minds of those involved. It does happen where crews attend a class on electrical hazards then make numerous mistakes mitigating an electrically charged transformer fire. Peer team analysis attempts to determine why correct knowledge wasn't used at an event. How can training be altered to ensure knowledge is usable at the next event?

New or Unfamiliar Equipment

Sometimes it is difficult to become familiar with new equipment. It may take time for the frontline to develop (unsanctioned but useful) workarounds or shortcuts for new equipment or technology. Given enough time and usage, familiarity with new equipment or technology results in decreases of operational distress. Don't be surprised if this results in more operational errors for a while.

Peer analysis should focus on why new equipment increased cognitive demands or made the work more difficult. Was there training for the new equipment or technology? How was competency determined? What consideration, or lack thereof, was given to the human-machine interface? New equipment considerations shouldn't increase cognitive demands once in place. In a perfect world, by the time it reaches the field, competency should be at the mastery level for all users.

Procedural Over-Adherence, Under-Adherence, and 'On the Fly' Adaptations

Procedures are tricky. We use terms like "operational guidelines" and "standard operating procedures" to describe how we should be doing things. These terms describe a wide spectrum of the detail needed to write them. Guidelines can be broad or general, whereas procedures are supposed to be very specific with more rigid adherence. What I have found is the frontline doesn't differentiate much between the two terms. They just want to know what you want them to do and how you want it done. They'll take it from there.

Peer analysis should include review of applicable OG/SOPs and a search for rigid adherence, noncompliance and adaptations that made sense to those involved in the event. Analysis also seeks to find a lack of applicable OG/SOPs.

In a large municipal department, an SOP related to modern fire behavior tactics stipulated the first arriving crew to an obvious working fire will lay a supply line, position as the primary pumper just past the front of the structure, don SCBAs, seek available information from witnesses about occupants, conduct a 360, establish IRIC, and determine the best anchor location for the initial attack.
For this department, 360s commonly ended up being some degree of a 180 as the list of tasks was almost unmanageable. Peers could relate to the time it took to perform all the above tasks and conduct

a full 360 while negotiating gates, fences, and unknown backyard animals. They noticed that it took so long that the interior attack was commenced by second due companies and that ventilation efforts were delayed. Instead of 360 evaluations, 180s became mutually acceptable between crews because no one cared to have their deployed hose lines pirated by another company.

We are all familiar with the uncomfortable feeling that we arrive first only to set the table for others to eat. Then get stuck with cleaning up and overhaul because our apparatus is buried on the street by lines and later arriving trucks. So, members can – and do over time – adjust their adherence to the procedures without going back and rewriting them. This sets the organization up for loss, sometimes catastrophic. This is practical drift as defined by Scott Snook.

Peer teams understand this pressure and other similar pragmatic drift movements over time. As they identify drift and other conflicting priorities, the issue of why should be uncovered as well as proposals for solutions as to how operational OG/SOPs or principals should be altered. Additionally, any internal movements of practical drift or the normalization of deviation can be made transparent and managed out in the open since it is likely past successes have reinforced all kinds of movement away from work as it is imagined by those who developed the OG/SOP.

Resilience Considerations

The following four factors help highlight resilience related issues. They can help make the transition into the creation of department wide shared findings since that is the principal outcome of conducting serious event reviews.

1) Response Sufficiency

Were the resources that were responding sufficient and properly typed for the type and scale of the event? Is the expectation or pride of the department found in doing more with less? If it is, then peers should ask themselves what behaviors or deeper assumptions promote or facilitate this type of resource management? Identify which OG/SOPs dictate response levels. Are mutual aid or automatic aid agreements being used to their full potential?

2) Relevant Indicators of Conditions

Determine which event indicators were known to those performing the actions. Have previous similar circumstances or events been identified and used in training? If not, why were they not seen as relevant enough for curriculum development and delivery? Why and how were relevant indicators either noticed or missed? Can controls be added to procedures or trained through drills to help filter for irrelevant indications?

3) Detection of Threats

Determine how organizational or system experience and training played either a negative or positive role in the event. What information was transferred from the call taker to mobile data terminals for units dispatched? Were relevant time indicators made known to all units and did they understand time's impact? Did the pressure of time impact evaluation of the threats and response to them? Did useful communications receive priority over other information? How did a low understanding of important threats impact resource management?

4) Learning and Long-Term Sustainability

Did the organization have a similar event where learning was missed or did not receive organizational support? Some organizations lack a process for ensuring previous calls or incidents are packaged and reviewed by all members. Is that the case here? Perhaps transparency is not valued, and learning is not the response of senior leadership. Do crews show up for training and education or is regularly scheduled training delayed or missed all together due to competing priorities, especially fiscal? Have past training and procedural changes been altered over time to fit into operations today?

This is not an all-inclusive list, but one to help new peer teams get started with the work of sensemaking and analysis and developing shared findings. It is helpful to keep track of your department's considerations over time, as they happen. SO/HSOs who can look back at previous analysis considerations will become well-equipped for the next incident review. As future review peer teams are formed, the experience of the facilitator is the only common thread between the last or next review.

Review Performance

Building a peer team must be done carefully and with consideration for those involved in the event (relationally and professionally). If your event is large or emotionally charged, find peer members with helpful leadership characteristics that keep things moving forward instead of stalling prior to goal achievement. I recommend asking for help from a neighboring department that has had peer review team training.

We tried different timing for conducting this phase. As I have mentioned before, it worked best for memory recall to conduct the discovery phase as soon as possible after the event. This also helps to put to good use the emotional energy available post adverse event. Once you are finished with the interviews, have the original interviews transcribed and take them with all the discovery information to your peer team. Plan on giving the peer team a few days to become acquainted with all the event factors including dispatch recordings of the event and the interview transcriptions.

With concern for mental and emotional well-being, the inner ring members may be asked to individually sit with the peer team to offer clarifications about the event context if they are requested. After the inner ring has sat with the peer team, questioning of outer ring members can come as a teams or groups. After questioning those involved, the peer team can add additional influence on the network of influences map related to the event. This exercise is designed to flush out contextual findings for the final sharing findings phase. Although it seems like it might take some time to map influences, I found it progresses quickly because the team makes the work easy. There is a tendency, a deep seated one, to review how one or two people failed to prevent the event.

Be careful not to allow the peer team to take the easy familiar method of blaming one or two people. Interestingly, the resilience of these old, tired tendencies is strong and doesn't go away easily. With each peer team, be sensitive to how past cultural tendencies draw teams back into familiar blame processes and hijack your SERT process.

Section Five Summation

Sensemaking and analysis attempts to determine how and why events transpired as they did. Why decisions made sense to those involved and what can be learned by others. It is not a phase for determining who should take responsibility for the event. Use of peers to analyze is helpful because the solutions they might help develop are more likely to be useful to those doing the work.

Some factors that commonly come up during this phase of the review are described in this section. Additionally, some resilience considerations are offered. Resilience considerations help the peer team consider how future work might become more flexible. Work can be done under newly adopted policies or procedures that add capacity to automatic response systems.

Mapping influential context is done initially by the review facilitators in the discover information phase and secondarily by the peer team in the sensemaking and analysis phase.

Questions to Consider

1. T or F: This second phase is the work of making sense of how or why things happened and what the essential learning points will be for your organization.

2. One of the goals in this phase is to:
a) Make work simple to do and efficient.
b) Make work difficult to do well and difficult to do incorrectly.
c) Make future work easy to do safely and harder to do unsafely.
d) Make future work hard to do.

3. The "stick to the plan no matter what" factor:
a) Is closely related to procedural over-adherence.
b) Means there is a lack of ongoing decision-making.
c) Assumes there is a well-thought-out plan that will work given enough time.
d) None of the above.

4. Good stress and bad stress are also called:
a) Duress and distress
b) Eustress and distress
c) Distress and duress
d) Uress and distress

5. Erroneous or inactive knowledge:
a) Is a result of poorly monitored academy training.
b) Is a result of uncontrolled OJT.

c) Can spread like a virus and impact a whole shift before it is caught by someone with expertise.
d) All the above.

6. When analyzing for resilience:
a) Include checking to see if the response was sufficient for the type of call.
b) Look for relevant indications of conditions that are shared and known to everyone.
c) Ensure times were known to everyone so threats could be detected early.
d) A and B.
e) All the above.

Section Six | Sharing Findings

Outcome Delivery

As the analysis and sensemaking phase is finalized, the final phase of the review process is to develop and deliver the narrative report to the Division/Deputy or Assistant Chief of the division in which the incident took place. I like to suggest the designated Chief assemble a small ad hoc team or ask a standing committee to review the report and help with the process of sharing findings with the rest of the organization. This phase is meant to build actions and share findings that will increase reliability and resilience. Initially, most chief officers (including civilian director-level staff) may feel a little intimidated by the process as it moves in their direction. SO/HSOs or designated review facilitators will continue facilitating the process by explaining the findings of the review thus far.

Two objectives need to be met. 1) A method for sharing findings will need to be determined, and 2) A written action plan for the findings and subsequent actions should be developed with the names of those responsible for the actions identified. Action plans will serve as an institutionalized document for your review outcomes.

Essentially, this phase is the final process where factors found in the sensemaking and analysis phase are considered and actions are agreed upon moving forward. Procedures, training, and education are reviewed and changed if needed. Communication to all members is planned with clear objectives. The obvious goal is to prevent similar adverse events from occurring. But the primary goal is to learn how the organization will increase consistency and capacity, reliability and resilience.

The example below contains an overview for an in-service training injury event with edited findings from the peer team's sensemaking and analysis where they held tightly to certain common analysis factors. Hopefully, this offers an overview of what the second phase moving into the third phase looks like in draft form. All identifiers are continually edited out to keep the focus of the findings on system needs not the individual(s). This also honors nondisclosure agreements when they are used.

Training Injury Example:

> Three Engine companies (two from the original FD and one from a neighboring FD), one Battalion Chief, and three training staff officers (from a neighboring FD) arranged to meet and videotape the deployment of specific hose loads for training purposes. Crews met at an occupied two-story garden apartment complex because it offered commonly encountered hose deployment obstructions, including stairs, and was the site of a very recent apartment fire on the second floor.

Several deployments of dry hose were performed while the training staff video-recorded the deployments. As crews conducted the hose evolutions, a side conversation about the past deployment results of the Cleveland load occurred. This conversation ultimately resulted in a decision to use air from an Engine's CAF system to compare deployments of an Accordion load and a Cleveland load. A 2.5-inch line was laid in a horizontal standpipe configuration from the CAF pumper about 200 feet to the training site, where a 2.5-inch to 1.75-inch gated wye was used to facilitate the use of two 1.75-inch hoses pressurized with just air from the compressor.

The Cleveland load was attached to the gated wye, and two members deployed it to the second-floor landing. After it was pressurized, it was depressurized by opening the bale on the handline, which was still connected to the now-closed gated wye. The same procedure was followed, and the Accordion load was pressurized, then deflated by opening the bale on the nozzle. Unfortunately, this may have given some firefighters a sense that the pressure was managed and not an issue.

Direction was given to "wrap it up" and return to a nearby station for more deployments using water. Both handlines were disconnected from the gated wye, and members collectively gathered up the hoses. One firefighter relieved the pressure in the 2.5-inch hose by opening one port of the gated wye. As it opened, a very loud "pop" was heard, and the hose, with the gated wye on the end, recoiled and whipped as it escaped from the grip of the firefighter. As it whipped uncontrollably, the gated wye struck two firefighters, resulting in an angulated, open compound fracture of the lower leg of one firefighter. It then struck the foot of another firefighter, tearing through the leatherwork of the shoe, bending the steel toe, causing a lower ankle injury, and knocking the firefighter to the ground. The hose was quickly subdued by a nearby firefighter, and the remaining pressure was relieved.

Analysis Outcome Report
Cognitive Analysis
- Time was a factor because the crews wanted to get back to the station and back in service. The decision to use air was a time-based decision because it was quicker and easier to clean up. Hazard analysis was not verbally articulated.
- Crews were fixated on trying to get training and comparison done and did not recognize the hazards they were placing around themselves.
- The decision to use air was made by persons considered the subject matter experts for this drill, which resulted in a bias for or toward their ability to manage the risks.
- The team agreed there are differences between what happens during a training environment versus a drilling environment at the company level. Fixation is more likely to result at company drilling versus Training Division trainings because the Training Division must meet applicable standards that regulate the larger training events and give hazard briefings before training is started.

Plan Analysis
- In the original plan, they were using dry, unpressurized hose; therefore, the team agreed that originally it was the right plan at that time. It was determined that the change to using air pressure at the end of the original training evolution was done quickly. The evidence of a serious hazard was not obvious or strong enough to alter the crew's thoughts about what had taken place. Additionally, the two evolutions with air were done quickly and were insufficient to warn members of the hazards.
- The crews decided to stick with the plan because they did not comprehend the differences between hydraulic and pneumatic pressure.
- The tradeoffs or costs if the plan had been abandoned may have resulted in more time spent picking up wet hose at an occupied apartment complex training site.
- The team agreed that there was an original plan, then a quick alteration without any real hazard briefing or adjustments of PPE.

Stress Analysis
- The team agreed that for the people in charge, the stress of running a timely drill may have been a factor, but not for the rest of the crews. Distress did not appear to be a factor.

Fatigue Analysis
- The team agreed that there was no evidence of tasks requiring sustained attention, cognitive, or memory issues. Fatigue was not a factor.

Knowledge Analysis
- The crews didn't fully comprehend the hazards and risks of using air instead of water. Use of air isn't a normal operation.
- The team agreed that there was incomplete understanding among the crews. Some had never seen air used before in a drill, whereas some members had once before.
- The team agreed that although there was an opportunity for a hazard briefing, it wasn't done because a thorough understanding of the potential for injury when using air, especially after numerous dry hose drills, air usage was assumed to be a useful alternative that fit the desired comparison of hose loads.
- The team found understanding of the hazard was considered more subjective rather than objective.
- Training with air pressure in hoses was rare, except for one high-rise drill and TRT drills. Knowledge about air pressure versus water pressure was not known.
- Crews did not possess specific knowledge about the difference between hydraulic and pneumatic pressure and how fast the air, with little friction loss, moves through the line.

Equipment Analysis
- The team agreed the incident that occurred was completely unexpected, but that the equipment performed to expectations. The addition of CAF systems some time ago was an automation improvement of firefighting capabilities. To no one's recollection on the team was there any consideration of training or discussions on the hazards associated with compressed air foam versus water in hoselines.

Procedures Analysis
- The crews treated and seemed to equate the use of compressed air to using water. There is no accepted practice or procedure for using compressed air in hose drills instead of water.
- Some accepted practices and procedures were violated. No qualified pump operator remained at the pump panel when the compressed air was used. Also, there was a lack of PPE for the members using pressurized hoses. The procedure used to bleed pressure from the gated wye was incorrect.
- Members of the public moved freely through an active drill site. Conducting safe training does not allow for the public to move around pressurized hoses or trip hazards. No specific procedure exists for managing the public, nor does one exist for company drill planning.
- The apartment manager was not notified of an extended drill activity on the premises.

Narrative Story Versus Timeline Diagram

The above report is a good example of how things should begin to take shape from the sensemaking analysis phase to the start of the share findings phase. I like the use of the narrative which gives just enough information about how the event occurred but does not give any value to a timeline or assume this event happened in a linear manner. I believe serious events, although they may seem linear, are complex with numerous influences. Most actions and behaviors are influenced by past, present, and future influencers all at the same time. Narratives offer flexibility to move within time instead of having to strictly adhere to it. Following timelines tends to miss how complex the event context was for those making decisions at the time.

In this case, I also find the desire for company training from the crews as well as the organization (BC's love to see crews out drilling) was not supported by the organization(s) that mandates in-service training. Company officers never had training on how to adequately prepare for on-shift company training. The fact that a firefighter made a mistake should not be the only focus.

Additionally, this event in narrative form does not take much time to present. I found the more time a review takes to present to the troops, the more the review will create goal conflicts (tension) with other deliverables in the organizational queue. Time in front of busy crews or at quarterly training is a premium.

Sharing Findings

When we chose to have BCs deliver findings at stations on shift, we found inconsistencies between what and how findings were emphasized to crews. On rare occasions, no delivery was the outcome due to call volume or new priorities interfering. Even when instructor notes were printed there were still delivery inconsistencies. There is considerable autonomy out in the field with fire departments. Autonomy can hinder or enhance all kinds of things. Be careful about how you deliver findings. Be sure to consider other means of delivery: PowerPoint, YouTube®, in-house videos, or station-to-station "road shows" by a designated team. Each one has its benefits, costs, and limitations. I cannot tell you what will work best for your organization. Numerous considerations go into each delivery method.

I suggest picking a means of delivery for the presentation to upper management and perhaps a different one for the frontline. Respectfully, upper management needs to receive a constant diet of review information which will translate into tailoring your presentations in a way that reinforces any or all the five HOP principles. Review findings will have upper management appeal when findings can be used to help stakeholders understand how things happen, how things are fiscally related, and how different preparations or controls can add or subtract resilience for the system.

If a layer or two of supervision exists between you and your senior staff or Fire Chief, expect any handoff for the delivery to a ranking member to cost the review in one way or another. It is not uncommon to have a senior ranking chief deliver what he or she thinks is important versus what the review team thought. Be careful with this one. Once again, priorities are interpreted differently depending on the person, time, and outside influential factors like politics, fiscal issues, social issues, and environmental issues.

The frontline delivery method needs considerable control of content and consistency of message. Use media and training record management programs to ensure viewing by all members but considerable resources, expertise, and time are necessary to deliver quality content that keeps firefighters and staff interested. Even though "road shows" out to the stations take considerable time to deliver, the face-to-face time with one or two people consistently doing the presentations is reliable and brings an ROI of organized feedback. Out-of-service quarterly training or captain's meetings are costly so make sure your delivery has been reviewed by senior staff and meets their expectations prior to the first training.

When high-profile adverse events take place, everyone will want to know what happened and what is being done to make sure it won't happen again. If upper management isn't invested in review program outcomes, then expect impatience from those who are unfamiliar with the process. As I've mentioned, the appetite for blame and its illusion of control is strong and doesn't ever really go away (resilient). The tendency toward certainty is strong, and some will struggle with patience as they wait for results.

Working with a division head or chief to determine how to disseminate the findings is straightforward. Most are grateful for the emphasis on learning instead of blaming. They want good morale, trust, and a safe workplace for their staff and firefighters. In large and small organizations, the training division may offer to integrate some review findings with future training they have planned. Reinforcement later is a great way to keep the emphasis on building resilience over time. Other divisions may also be willing to do some integration as well. Walking the scrubbed (no identifiers) review findings around after the analysis has merit because it offers opportunity to consolidate solutions.

After meeting with the designated chief or ad hoc team a rough draft action plan should emerge that lists actions to take and who will be responsible for them. Deadlines are added but leave that discussion up to the upper-level managers. As an SO/HSO you are tasked with facilitating the review. Organizational leaders need to adjust priorities all the time so leave action plan timelines up to the Fire Chief.

Below is a list of developing recommendations from the prior training accident event prior to being entered into a task plan. Ask yourself which items below are low-hanging fruit and which ones will need to be added to the strategic plan due to resource needs.

Firefighter Injury Review – Action Plan (Draft)

Operations
- Eliminate public access to all drill sites.
- Reinforce mandatory use of PPE when drill site or fire ground has hazardous energies present.
- Task equipment committee with researching gated wye improvements.
- Widen scope of equipment committee to include communicating hazards of new approved tools.
- Evaluate and make recommendation for shutting off all remaining CAF systems.

Training
- Address the lack of close call reporting in all divisions.
- Officer training that includes how time pressures influence decision-making during drills, and how to vet training before it takes place.
- Train on use of drill checklist for future company drills.
- Work with Fire Maintenance division on recommendations for pump operator training on management of hazardous energies and constant presence at pump panels.
- Develop new procedure for safe handling and a universal method for bleeding pressure from hose lines.

Fire Maintenance
- Eliminate use of air pressure in hoses on the fire ground when clearing hoses of foam.

You will notice there are additional actions to take outside of the earlier findings. This is a normal outcome of a good peer team that captured additional context related to the "how" of this incident. This event led to a great deal of discussion about gated wyes. Eventually gated wyes were removed from apparatus due to a similar close call when one was accidentally kicked open as it lay underneath a thick layer of foam on the fire ground, and due to the physics encountered when two lines are operating and one shuts down.

Compressed air systems were becoming obsolete due to foam technologies evolving, so shutting off the remaining systems was an obvious choice. But the recognition of pressure hazards was heightened by this event, which was a plus for continued management of pressurized hose lines at fire scenes and training. The action item about close call reporting came from the analysis team discovering similar close calls in training environments that met close call parameters but were not reported at the time of the event. Hence, the decision to have the Training Division manage the close call reporting educational component.

Section Six Summation

Shared findings will be delivered to the Division, Deputy or Assistant Chief of the functional area in which the event took place. It is up to the designated Chief to assemble a team, or not, to review the analysis findings and determine what needs to be done in an action plan. Two objectives need to be met. One, a mechanism for delivery needs to be decided on. Two, a plan needs to be written and circulated to everyone who will have responsibilities in the action plan. The Fire Chief should give final approval.

All findings and action plan items need to be vetted against the backdrop of whether they will help prevent a future similar occurrence, increase consistency and reliability, and increase capacity and resilience.

It is recommended sensemaking and analysis findings are placed in a narrative form as the analysis phase is wrapping up. This method of communicating is usually faster and more representative of how events transpired outside of some linear framework.

Delivery of findings can be tricky. By the time the process is ready to deliver findings, the organization has probably been pressed on to other priorities. It is possible the review findings and action plan will compete for time and energy. Picking a reliable method for delivery is key. Take care making this choice. The review findings may look different for you command staff versus the front line, so the delivery may also be different.

Questions to Consider

1. Analysis findings should be reviewed by
a) The individual(s) who created the event.
b) The division head of the division responsible for the HSO.
c) The division head of the division the event took place in.
d) The division head of the person who created the event.

2. Two objectives in the share findings phase need to be met. They are
a) Determine a method of delivery
b) A written action plan needs to be developed
c) Someone will have to rewrite policies and procedures.
d) B and C
e) A and B

3. T or F   The obvious goal of a review is to prevent future occurrences. The primary goal is to learn how the organization will increase reliability and resilience.

4. T or F   Using a timeline to explain an adverse event tends to miss how complex the event context was for those making decisions.

5. What would be a benefit of using "road shows" as a review delivery method?
a) Consistency of message
b) Feedback regarding the frontline's responses.
c) Both A and B
d) Neither A nor B

Section Seven | Newer Perspectives on Safety

As we explore modern approaches to safety management, Todd Conklin, Ph.D. advocates for redefining safety not as "the absence of harmful or adverse events," but as "the presence of defenses." For the fire service this translates into a new paradigm: safety is not merely the absence of accidents, but the active presence of capacity to manage or soften failures.

Safety gains derived from monitoring and improving human behaviors often plateau. When accident and injury rates stabilize at lower, but consistent levels, organizations face a choice: accept these new levels or recognize that these metrics don't fully define a safety program or prevent catastrophic events. The recommended path here is to move toward deeper understanding and find ways to create greater reliability and resilience.

This transition requires time and may encounter organizational influences that can stall progress or lead to uncertainty. A program's journey is susceptible to both internal and external factors, extending beyond common influences like economics or politics. Below are some common factors every SO/HSO might consider as they implement a review program that seeks to learn versus blame individuals or small groups.

People Help *and* Hinder

Fortunately, firefighters within the same department often perform tasks differently, even when adhering to identical procedures. This variability in performance is rich with adaptations — necessary adjustments made to effectively complete work under uncertain and changing conditions. This is a major part of your organization's resilience.

Consider this scenario:

> An engine company and ambulance respond to a call just after midnight to a large 10-lane freeway where motorists are traveling at 75-85 mph. No law enforcement is on the scene. A motorist has pulled to the right shoulder, reporting increasing difficulty breathing. The apparatus is strategically angled to block the shoulder creating a safe work zone while the ambulance is parked upstream with doors open for gurney removal. As the company officer what is the best course of action?
>
> A) Quickly remove the patient from the car and transfer them to the ambulance without the gurney, full vitals, or assessment, then assess and treat enroute to the hospital.
> B) Obtain a full set of vitals in the patient's vehicle, bring the gurney close to the driver's side door, then move the patient to the ambulance and treat enroute to the hospital.

While many other factors are at play or may need to be considered, this example highlights that firefighters understand medical algorithms but may adapt their operations, weighing productivity, resources, and safety differently. Environmental context can override standard patient care protocols, depending on real-time firefighter perceptions. We rely on firefighters to make these critical, on-the-spot decisions. Every call involves balancing production, efficiency, and safety. Addressing trouble breathing on a 10-lane freeway is different from trouble breathing in a living room recliner.

Without elaborate recognition firefighters typically execute tasks successfully and move on. This continuous adjustment is a core strength of your department's human element. Firefighters are the resource that provide operational flexibility. When staffing is low, they compensate; when danger increases, they adjust their pace; when call volume is high, they increase production efficiency; and when it's low they increase thoroughness. They inherently know how and when to make necessary tradeoffs.

To truly understand both effective and less effective variations, reviews are essential. The primary function of a review should be to clarify how and why actions made sense when they were performed. When work is successful, reviews should assess performance variations and human interventions, making situational complexity transparent for collective learning. When an adverse event occurs, reviews should focus on understanding the full context of factors that influenced behaviors and choices.

Jens Rasmussen, Ph.D. raises a critical concern regarding limitations, "The concept of human error is very elusive. At a closer look, the frequent allocation of accidental causes to human error appears to be subjective and guided by the toolbox of the analyst. This is a simple reflection of the nature of causal analysis and the fact that no objective stop rule exists to terminate the causal backtracking in search of a root cause. The search stops when an event is found for which a cure is known to the analyst." [35]

Dr. Rasmussen highlights two key points here. First, many investigators tend to stop their inquiry prematurely when an easy or common corrective action becomes apparent. This is a result of limited or poor investigative training, and it results in limited reach into deeper systemic issues — such as culture, funding, political pressures, or resource management — which remain unaddressed. Second, he reveals that human error is not as straightforward as it initially may seem. An investigator's perspective is inherently subjective, often biased by their training and methodology, leading to findings that may reinforce existing biases rather than uncover deeper truths.

Human error is often overstated as a cause of an adverse event. Even worse, root cause can be attributed to broader cultural or organizational issues, which overstates the scope of root cause entirely. It is often simpler to cease deeper investigation and blame individuals as cultural influences are dynamic and challenging to pinpoint. The aim of this text and related course is to prevent the fire service from conducting low-quality reviews due to a lack of proper training and understanding.

---

[35] Pre-Accident Investigations, An Introduction to Organizational Safety, T. Conklin, Ashgate Publishing, Surrey England, 2012.

Psychological Safety

Psychological safety, as a practice, is defined as:
> "A belief that one will not be punished or humiliated for speaking up with ideas, questions, concerns or mistakes, and that the team is safe for interpersonal risk-taking."
> – Amy Edmondson

The pursuit of safer operations on the pre-accident side of the equation is influenced by whether a sense of psychological safety exists or not. If a firefighter doesn't think psychological safety exists, they are less likely to invest and make contributions about team operational improvements. Operational safety stop statements like, "it takes four to go and one to say no" are not taken seriously.

Psychological safety is a core principle that helps an organization move from retributive to restorative practices. Psychological safety is cultivated through trained company officers and battalion chiefs providing and maintaining environments where it is safe to speak up. As culture evolves toward valuing psychological safety, SO/HSOs will build on the increased level of trust and attain higher levels of participation and feedback.

After an accident the presence of psychological safety allows firefighters to speak up without fear of retribution, loss of credibility, or being seen as a target to be humiliated (frequently with clever humor). Leadership and labor need to stop human error or blame processes so everyone can account for their actions under the context that they experienced. Maintaining privacy, discouraging some of the clever humor, scrubbing reports of names (any identifiers), and NDAs signed by reviewers and those doing analysis are all practices that move the dial toward psychological safety.

Success

In his book, *The Black Swan*,[36] Nassim N. Taleb recounts the story of a turkey fed daily for 1,000 days. The turkey, relying on this consistent meal plan (data) either naively assumes its immortality or faces the shocking reality of becoming Thanksgiving dinner. Our motivations to prepare for the uncertain calls in the fire service often mirror the turkey's choices. We might assume past success guarantees future positive outcomes and become what appears to be something akin to complacent. Or, we might reject this subjective belief and remain vigilant, actively preparing for unpredictable factors.

Alarmingly, I've observed reliability decline at the company level following periods of success. I think we grow comfortable, numbed to risks, and cease striving for continuous improvement believing we've "arrived"— much like the turkey fed daily. While some managers label this as complacency, it's often a deeper issue of missed leadership preparation for how success conditions us. What's also troubling is our collective failure to critically analyze the successes we do experience. Success frequently contains

---

[36] *The Black Swan, The Impact of the Highly Improbable*; N. Taleb, Random House Inc., New York, (2010) pg. 186.

elements of failure, offering valuable lessons. Because these failures were overcome, I believe failures within successful operations hold gold nuggets of resilience we can use to build reliability.

We universally dedicate far more resources to reviewing failure events versus our successes. Successful operations often receive informal tailboard critiques lacking formal organizational feedback. Larger, multi-alarm successes might warrant a post-incident review (PIR) if time and resources allow. We are conditioned to investigate why we failed, not why we succeeded. Yet, successful operations are precisely where we should seek the reliability and resilience characteristics we want in our organizations. This holds true for every aspect of our work: in the shop, alarm room, technical services, training, and EMS.

The term "success-engendered optimism," discussed in section one, is pertinent here. Success naturally fosters a subjective belief — personally and organizationally — that more success will follow. This subjective belief is dangerous. When decisions on calls come more from belief rather than objective assessment, catastrophic failure becomes a real risk. It's crucial not to dismiss inaction or failure as mere complacency, as it often warrants deeper investigation. Complacency carries a negative, blaming connotation whereas success-engendered optimism acknowledges past achievements while still pointing to a potential blind spot that goes beyond any single individual who made a mistake.

One of the best company officers I worked with was never content waiting for the next quarterly training. His crew trained daily, and their preparedness was evident on calls. He understood that consistent preparation was key to counteracting subjective optimism. Kudos to those who persistently push their BCs/DCs for more out-of-service training time. Keep it up! Similarly, SO/HSOs are responsible for guiding frontline personnel away from the subjective belief of being good enough. They must foster objective readiness through ongoing training. Sharing internal stories of close calls where success-engendered optimism almost led to catastrophe can effectively communicate the stark choice; be prepared or become tomorrow's dinner.

Falling on the Sword

It's never if, but when an accident or serious event will happen. When it does, how do your people respond to an error made by one of your members? Do other firefighters shun them and say, "I would have never done that." Do they respond empathetically and show compassion for those responsible? There are indeed many possibilities and leaders hold the power to take the organization in a learning trajectory. However, and I hope you agree, the fire service in general tends to want to know what happened and feels some compassion for most of our firefighters who are involved in adverse events resulting in high-visibility failure. This is a good start, but without leadership's commitment to restorative practices, blame may become a secretive and seductive option, especially when various elements of credibility and control are at stake.

For most error events resulting in failure, accountability is determined depending on some combination of HR's understanding of the relatable rules, Labor's take on whether the rules were applicable (if even written), an attorney's opinion, and the Fire Chief's ability to find balance while protecting reputations. In most cases, a great deal of closed-door energy will be expended determining who is responsible and how much corrective action or punishment is required. We may end up thinking we are fortunate when someone steps forward and takes responsibility by "falling on the sword."

In my experience, it is common for firefighters to accept responsibility for failure and success. An organization might think how fortunate it is that someone stepped forward with reasons that range from "I didn't know" to "I made an honest mistake." Sometimes, the reasons for a courageous *mea culpa* can be heroic. They may want to keep others clear of trouble, hope that coming forward early will mean a lighter sentence, or just want to get past all this and move on. At times, they assume they made the mistake – even though they may not be sure. Whatever the reason, when the mistake isn't intentional (during some operations there were only bad choices left to make) I believe the best response to them is to say, "Thanks, now let's begin to understand what made your actions seem right to you at the time." The organization should seize the opportunity to launch a fair and curious discovery process so we can all learn.

Someone admitting guilt or taking responsibility is not the end of a review. It is the beginning of the search for relevant context surrounding the decision(s) at the time of the event. Don't sell the greater mission of learning short by thanking these brave souls for their courage in coming forward and calling a stop to the investigation/review so corrective actions can be drawn up.

And to keep things in balance, our courageous firefighters willing to take the blame also have a responsibility to help everyone understand why their decisions seemed like good ones at the time and what influenced them. This is what's meant by making context and decisions transparent which is the only way I know of to combat the growing complexity within our systems.

Black Lines, Blue Lines (and Red)

There is a difference between work as it is planned and work as it is performed. Another way I've heard this concept stated is, "work as imagined is not work as it is done." Either way, plans and OG/SOPs are wonderful until they get used, then they start to take on a host of new priority conflicts, influences, personalities, and environments. Work as it is imagined is not work under normal conditions. It may help to use the illustration below (Figure 7).

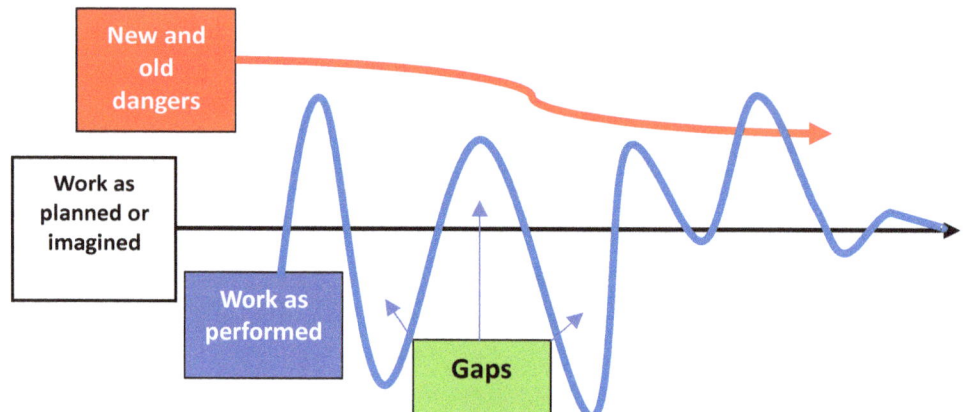

Figure 7 Work as Imagined vs. Work as Performed

The black line represents how we plan or imagine work happening. The blue line represents how work is actually getting done with day-to-day variances. The red line represents dangers that develop over time at active incidents as firefighters work. The green box represents operational gaps that open between what is planned and what really happens on any call or assignment. Gaps are operational disparities between how work is designed and how work is really getting done. They occur more than we'd care to admit. Let's look at an example.

Close Call Narrative

>The setting was an early morning fire hidden in the floors and walls of a wooden residential structure that finally, after enough time and air, evolved from light white haze upon arrival, to thick black smoke, then to flash over and free burning. Considerable time had elapsed as the IC received reports from interior crews that they were making progress. In the background of radio transmissions, the IC could hear chainsaw sounds, which made him/her feel comfortable the crews were gaining access and making progress.
>
>In reality, the chainsaw sounds were firefighters with one saw making relatively small floor cuts over and around metal floor beams, while another saw sat idling on the floor. Additionally, unknown to the IC, a piercing nozzle had become stuck in one of the metal beams and it couldn't be dislodged, so water was not being distributed through the openings or any other piercings. The fire grew as exterior crews became naturally

impatient and opened exterior walls out of view of the IC due to the increasing smoke laying down from the morning atmospheric inversion.

Due to elapsed time and growing smoke production, the IC called for everyone to exit the structure. As the last exiting captain was evacuating, visibility was completely lost, hose lines were crisscrossed inside on the floor, and heat increased incredibly fast. The captain made a wrong turn, which left him/her disoriented. As he/she reached for a radio to call Mayday, a window was felt above and used to bail out on the ground floor in the rear of the structure. No Mayday was called. No one even knew a bail out had occurred because of smoke production. The roll call had just been started as the captain joined his/her crew in front of the structure.

The black line in this close call is represented by everyone bringing all the right tools, water supply, and sufficient staffing to the interior of the fire. A primary search was completed and the risk-benefit model moved toward less risk with more emphasis on the timer. With the verbal communications and confirming background sounds all was assumed to be moving toward fire control (work as imagined having effect). As time progressed the IC called for an evacuation to regroup, which appeared to be without any complications (again, work as imagined).

The blue line was two interior crews pulling out all the stops to reduce damage because when they arrived at this elderly occupant's house, they only had a light haze on the interior. They created small saw openings to locate and extinguish fire. They intended to use the piercing nozzle to gain access to shallow subfloor areas to extinguish fire. The nozzle got stuck in a metal beam, but the company officer didn't know. Two firefighters struggled unsuccessfully to dislodge the nozzle. As smoke intensified and darkened, exterior crews, without IC knowledge, turned their efforts to opening exterior walls. The initial efforts should have worked and created less damage to the structure, but due to the nozzle becoming stuck, another hose line was retrieved to replace the stuck nozzle (work as it is done).

Dangers encroached on fire operations as interior and exterior tasks resulted in fire growth instead of extinguishment. Quickly, on a logarithmic curve, the fire made the interior untenable (the red line). This result rarely happens, but at this residential fire, it did. Fortunately, the IC became very uncomfortable with the timer and the visually worsening conditions, so he/she called for an evacuation. As everyone was exiting a Captain accidentally separated from his/her crew and became disoriented. The separated Captain, due to training, stayed in contact with a wall and located a bail out window. He/she volunteered the close call experience to the Safety Captain later. This call ended up being a great reinforcement of the work as imagined compared to work as performed concept, especially for chief officers and company officers and the need for constant communication on all levels.

As learning continues, everyone understands work isn't often done exactly as it is imagined, so a new expectation is set where higher degrees of communication become necessary. What ends up being said to everyone isn't just about poor communication. It ends up being about how work deviates from how it was designed (which can be appropriate) to what was being done to get things done for our citizens. No one is at fault. It's just humans adjusting to meet perceived demands. But it must be communicated.

As the blue line (firefighters) adapts to the changing environments, they may knowingly or unknowingly cross over into dangerous work territory where risks may be difficult to recover from and an accident or injury event can take place. From the leadership level the error event looks like someone was not following procedure when, in fact, they were doing normal work and something understandable to their peers. Reducing the damage for the senior homeowner was, in the minds of the operating companies, more heroic than becoming bulls in the China shop.

To add to the interesting review findings of this close call, it was noted a firefighter who understood interior operations weren't going well didn't feel comfortable speaking up because he/she wasn't as familiar with their new company officer. Psychological safety was not as present as anyone would have hoped. Of course, we all wish this wasn't the case, but the experience speaks to the power of cultural environments at the company level and individual dispositions about authority.

Firefighters are always adapting to the needs and pressures of the moment. They bring adaptation and flexibility to the work placed before them. Operational environments need the human touch along with operational guidelines, otherwise operations become too brittle. In failure, success, and operations with close calls, there is a considerable amount of learning to be found in the operational gaps. Try not to miss them.

A helpful principle is to look for information from frontline workers after successful work. Post-event reviews reinforce the desire to learn from successful actions even though they may not have followed procedures. Successful actions may point to procedural changes and training that is needed to ensure safer operations organizationally.

In the book *Pre-Accident Investigations*, author Todd Conklin offers four post-job questions that will start the hunt for operational gap discrepancy understanding:[37]

>What happened the way you thought it would happen?
>What surprised you?
>What hazards did we identify and what hazards did we miss?
>Where did you have to "make do," improvise, or adapt?

---

[37] *Pre-Accident Investigations, An Introduction to Organizational Safety*, T. Conklin, Ashgate Publishing, Surrey England, 2012. Pg.40

Seeking Zero

Accident and injury numbers can easily end up representing the safety of an organization. If this is the case, the effort to reduce injuries or accidents to zero may be seen as a noble cause. This noble endeavor may misappropriate a lot of valuable energy and time. Commonly, accidents and injuries happen and instead of looking for context or goal conflict a report highlighting some form of human error is offered to leadership as an explanation. It almost feels like, in exasperation, we are saying, "Chief, we just can't get everyone to behave and stay in line." The desire to reestablish the zero-program goal then gets a doubling-down effort. It's a frustrating cycle that will deflate well-intentioned SO/HSOs trying to improve safety for their organization.

Although we want to eliminate accidents and injuries, zero programs can torpedo other good safety programs. I believe safety programs should seek information pertaining to what's really going on "in the wild." A deliberate effort on behalf of labor and management to support all efforts to report every type and severity of accident or injury without concern for fault is a great start. The new goal of record-keeping should be understanding work through accident, injury and close call reports without blame or retribution.

Truthfully, having zero reports does not mean your organization is safer or less likely to suffer a catastrophic event. In fact, it is not uncommon to have firefighters report less to help reach the zero goal which in turn hides real safety conflicts. The fewer the reports, the less the opportunity to build capacity into the system.

What is rarely a fundamental understanding to SO/HSOs is that organizational systems are always in some stage of degradation at any given time. Charles Perrow, in his book *Normal Accidents*, reviews numerous accidents in varying industries demonstrating that systems are dynamic. They are evolving and devolving, and they are not always understood by their operators.[38] Ever-changing system complexities make chasing zero reportable accidents much like rearranging deck chairs on the Titanic. Goal zero makes for good optics, but your proverbial ship is taking on water.

---

[38] *Normal Accidents, Living with High-Risk Technologies*, C. Perrow, Princeton University Press, New Jersey, 1999.

Chasing zero can also undermine other more important objectives. Every safety program needs as much data as the frontline will entrust to it. The more firefighters report, the more they are showing their trust and buy-in of safety program goals to build reliability and resilience. If they withhold information important data is lost about the organizational system. Everyone should want to know how the system is degrading or improving, 24/7.

Signals of failure whether ever so small, dormant, or only known by your frontline or support staff, are vying for attention all the time. SO/HSOs can expand the organizational sense of safety to include hunting for even the weakest failure signals, especially during successful operations where failures were overcome. SO/HSOs should look for ways to increase conversation with the frontline and support staff. Spend time doing informal meet and greets with your frontline and learn about what is happening during everyday operations.

Casual conversations will uncover a considerable amount of unintentionally hidden deviation that incrementally became normal operations over time. Normal deviation is a weak signal of compensatory behavior for a reason. The organization has a duty to uncover the reason and develop solutions. Seeking zero programs conflict with the forward-facing accountability duty every organization must hunt for weak signals of conflicting priorities that are precursors to failure.

Accident and injury reports only tell us what happened at a given moment. They describe a very small data point, a single episode, a moment often rich in context, that will never happen again. Rarely, if ever are two accidents or injuries the same. One FF sprained their ankle getting into the truck, while another sprained theirs getting off the truck. Don't spend too much time or energy on this smaller stuff. Hunt for the context and outliers and move on. Consider spending more time looking at successful outcomes where you may discover things like good lighting, three points of contact, or turning around and backing down the steps, to be objective prevention measures for ankle injuries. Then spec your apparatus appropriately as your program moves forward.

Tracking and Reporting

Accident and injury reports create records to support things like SCBA use is up, hand burn injuries are down and hopefully how reduction of exposure to toxins and carcinogens will decrease cancer rates for retiring firefighters 10-20 years from now. When reporting is done well, information may show a need to add controls to protect members from harmful elements under a given set of circumstances. Use reporting to encourage or sometimes discourage change. Reports are feedback. Reports are data. Collect data and offer meaningful feedback when you can.

Reports can guide early organizational safety efforts and supply program data. NFPA 1550 *Standard on Fire Department Occupational Safety, Health, and Wellness Program*[39] is a good start. NFPA 1550 has

---

[39] *NFPA 1550 Standard on Fire Department Occupational Safety, Health, and Wellness Program,* 2024 Edition, National Fire Protection Association, Quincy, MA 02169

a great deal of connection to other standards that will develop and challenge any department's effort to develop more reliable operating and logistical practices. A departmental goal with annual reports that express whether your department's efforts meet or exceed NFPA 1550 is foundational to setting a trajectory for increased capacity at the response level.

Supported by leadership and regulatory agencies, accident and injury numbers are regularly requested, and everyone should continue to report them. As an SO, I reported those numbers in my effort to meet or exceed standards. I also thought the numbers had more value than what I now believe. I used to think, depending on internal trends, we were either becoming safer or had more work to do shoring up deficiencies. Now, not as much. Don't let statistical spikes, outliers, or bell curves cause your blood to boil. They are just records that need to be managed so decisions about future reliability efforts can be based on experience, not someone's gut feeling. Be careful your practice of tracking and reporting accidents does not become a primary measurement of the presence of safety in your organization.

Despite data's limitations don't slack on tracking your data. It still can help you make strategic decisions for your safety program. If you do a poor job of tracking, you might end up making tactical and strategic decisions based on your gut instincts because the data was so poorly executed. The old saying, "garbage in, garbage out" might become your story. If our data is carefully recorded it could help with broader fire service projects where we all might collectively discover, on a national scale, how to improve operations or training.

As an example, researchers looked at over 65 emergency service vehicle incident articles that focused on what types of interventions had effectiveness in reducing accidents. Based on very limited outcome data (the key concept here) from just a handful of the articles, hands-on driver training was one of the best interventions for reducing accidents. This ended up being a very small dataset so it's important to understand the measurement may not carry much weight. In other words, we might end up shooting from the hip, not taking aim.

The second-overall best intervention, based on the same limited dataset, was proactive risk management. This supported the traditional approach to risks where risk is identified, evaluated, ranked, and controls are implemented. The value of searching (post-intervention) accident and injury numbers to substantiate a specific intervention's impact on outcomes could have been more useful as it relates to emergency vehicle safe operations. But unfortunately, most agencies submitting articles (data) couldn't demonstrate effect, good or bad, because they didn't have reliable accounting of accident rates. Reporting inconsistencies were the common factor.[40] Collectively we all missed an opportunity to look at ourselves and develop a reasonable solution due to local reporting limitations.

When recording accident and injury numbers break them down into detailed subparts. Ankle injuries should be described by work activity, left or right, footwear, time of day, previous work activities, and

---

[40] Bui DP, Balland S, Giblin C, Jung AM, Kramer S, Peng A, Aquino MCP, Griffin S, French DD, Pollack Porter K, Crothers S, Burgess JL. *Interventions and controls to prevent emergency service vehicle incidents: A mixed methods review*. Accid Anal Prev. 2018 Jun; 115:189-201. doi: 10.1016/j.aap.2018.01.006. Epub 2018 Apr 2.

number of work hours/days off due to the injury. Report consistently, then watch for activities that are influencing your rates. I found a couple of physical training activities resulting in considerable lost time. Recordkeeping efforts paid off when we implemented solutions and showed improvements.

Here is a positive example:
> A department had vehicle accident rates drop after implementation of a task book-type approach to driver training. There was a considerable amount of preparation, coaching, and testing of competency before members were certified to drive. The result overall was a drop in accident rates over time. Due to the size of the department, it took nearly three years to move everyone through the program.
>
> Detailed accident reports offered the ability to compare accidents against the constant of fleet miles driven as monitored by the city's refueling program, and code two versus code three accidents. Every 100,000 fleet miles, they could evaluate accident rates. Even as the number of vehicles increased due to growth, they continued to make the simple comparisons.
>
> Much later, as civilian-staffed ambulances were added to the fire department fleet under a new medical transport program, fleet accident rates increased compared to miles driven. The department SO could see the challenge clearly and noted the accidents were ambulances, code two, low speed, in close quarters. Now the effort to build the solution(s) could commence.

Section Seven Summation

Firefighters are a great resource. On calls they are continually adjusting to changing situations and balance the scales between efficiency, production, and safety. Mostly, they operate successfully. But on rare occasions (compared to the amount of work) mistakes cannot be overcome and the outcome is some form of failure. Reviews are a necessary component of fire department organizational self-critique of both successful and unsuccessful operations. Honest self-critique brings the kind of humble inquiry all organizations need to manage operational safety.

A necessary characteristic of reliable organizations building resilience into their systems is psychological safety. All members of the organization need to feel comfortable speaking up. If threats to reputation are perceived, most firefighters will withhold information because the personal risk is not worth the undetermined gain. This is most especially true when considering minor threats to operations that over time develop into catastrophic loses. Training and education on providing psychological safety for company officers and chief officers is a worthwhile investment from the perspective of safety programing.

Success can seductively lure company officers and crews into the subjective feeling that they are better than others or better than what they really are. This is a common phenomenon where almost everyone has varying degrees of unconscious susceptibility. It can be the reason why some people seem complacent when they probably wouldn't be if they understood what was really going on at deeper assumption levels. Using review findings to demonstrate when subjective beliefs have replaced objective reasoning is necessary if success engendered optimism is at work in your organization. Chief officers are just as likely to fall prey to this subjective optimism.

Don't let your firefighters think that falling on the sword is the end of the investigation. Especially if they really can't recall what happened or what they did. Someone admitting fault is only the beginning of learning from any event. Kindly accept their confession and then move on to learn from the event. Taking blame may diffuse some of the event emotion but it is not helpful learning.

Work as imagined is initial work design. Work as performed is work as it gets done. There is often a measurable difference. When officers understand this, they should actively seek differences to highlight after the incident. Spend time understanding exactly what took place and report the deviation from how work was imagined and how work was done. One of the best methods of resilience building is to combat the issue of how work design is different from work performance. A high degree of communication is necessary. Company officers need to make efforts to describe what they are doing.

SO/HSOs that work to achieve zero accidents may be doing themselves a disservice. Rewarding or encouraging zero reportable accidents/injuries will likely result in cutting off the information flow of how work is getting done and what is really going on out in the wild. I don't recommend zero programs and instead I advocate for reporting everything without penalty. Don't worry about anyone else having better accident rates or more employees with accident-free years. It holds very little value to those of us in emergency services who manage ourselves in an endless variety of environments and circumstances created by others.

Lastly, be sure to track the details of what gets reported and be consistent. It is hard to determine when or what information will be useful down the road. You may also want to share the data (with proper permissions) with other fire departments in your region as you help each other out. Perhaps with enough data your local university graduate programs may want to conduct some helpful research.

Questions to Consider

1. Firefighters adapt operationally weighing which factors based on their perceptions?
a) Safety
b) Productivity
c) Resources
d) A, B and C
e) A and C only

2. Which factors exert pressure on every call?
a) Fiscal
b) Production
c) Safety
d) All the above
e) A and C only

3. The "objective stop rule" has to do with
a) Stopping for all red lights regardless of the call type.
b) The point at which rules are no longer used in an SOP.
c) When a review is stopped due to legal constraints.
d) When an investigator drills down then stops looking any further.

4. T or F   Human error tends to get overstated as a root cause where deeper inquiry might have found cultural or organizational issues to be more causal.

5. Psychological safety is a concept partially defined as
a) The belief no one will be punished for speaking up
b) A feeling that this work environment is safe to work in
c) A sense no one is trying to get into your head to figure out if you know what's wrong.
d) The social perception that we can work safely together.

6. T or F   Psychological safety is a concept to pursue for any organization that is moving from retributive to restorative practices overall.

7. T or F   Success engendered optimism generally means our past successes will give us a sense that we will continue to be successful in the future. This general sense is subjective.

8. T or F   Someone "falling on the sword" generally means the investigation is over because someone has admitted guilt.

9. Work as imagined
a) Is generally the way things always get done.
b) Is rarely considered to be valuable.
c) Is not always how work gets done.
d) Creates gaps in new and old dangers

10. T or F   To overcome the minor and major discrepancies in black line - blue line actions, crews and incident commanders need to develop higher expectations for communications.

11. T or F   There are no issues with a department pursuing "zero accidents" programs.

12. T or F   Regarding tracking and trending, reporting consistency is one of the most important qualities of a good system.

Concluding Consideration

In 2014-15, using video footage (head-mounted cameras) researchers from Cardiff University and the Chief Fire and Rescue Officer Association of the UK found evidence that informed operational decision-making <u>did not</u> follow normal decision processes.[41] The study was an attempt to understand decision-making processes to help with future operational training development.

What they observed was that decision-making on the fire ground did not follow the normative decision-making process of 1) assessing the situation 2) formulating plans, then 3) executing the plan. They observed that situational assessment was followed by the execution of a plan, not the formulation of a plan (this supports Dr. Klein's work mentioned in Section One). They noted very little observation of incident commanders considering the consequences of actions taken. Incidents across six departments were studied.

The study concluded, "Decision-making did not follow the sequence of phases assumed by normative models and conveyed in current educational and operational guidance, but instead was influenced by both reflective and reflexive processes."[42] The application of their findings has "clear implications for understanding operational decision-making as it occurs in situ [in original place] and suggests a need for future guidance and training to acknowledge the role of reflexive processes."[43]

Before we move on here, let's clarify what the words reflective and reflexive mean. Reflective is used to describe decisions that follow the normative model of situational assessment, plan formulation, and plan execution. Reflexive is used to describe decisions that follow a shorter heuristic (learned mental shortcut) model of situational assessment, then plan execution, even though the plan may not be optimum.

Although both reflective and reflexive decision models were observed, the most common model used by far was reflexive, by both experienced officers and less experienced officers. This brings us to a rather uncomfortable thought: <u>If current reflective decision-making training and testing are used least often, do current training models and systems contribute to any of the consequential outcomes the fire service experiences?</u> Are we learning in a manner that supports common on-scene thought processes?

---

[41] Cohen-Hatton, Sabrina Rachel, Butler, Philip C. and Honey, Robert Colin ORCID: https://orcid.org/0000-0001-6870-1880 2015. An investigation of operational decision making in situ: Incident command in the UK Fire and Rescue Service. Human Factors 57 (5), pp. 793-804.

[42] ibid
[43] ibid

Could it be true that an investment in the development of training methods that support reflexive decision-making might mean better training for our incident commanders, mechanics, dispatchers and paramedics? Specifically, internally experienced and learned simulations and storytelling? Perhaps as we learn from our operations in a narrative fashion, the data collected will offer meaningful material for simulations and storytelling which would contribute to better reflexive decision-making at incidents.

To optimize reflexive event decisions, developmental training could create real-time scenarios where decisions can be practiced and reviewed until competency is gained. In a primitive form, this training is performed in current command-setting environments with radio feedback (players) that use scene photos or short videos to make the command environment seem more real.

However, new realities of artificial intelligence (AI), virtual reality (VR), augmented virtual reality (AVR), improvements to haptics in immersive training and web-based education platforms are here. The time for the fire service to make immersive training a priority is now. The case has been made that our model of decision-making needs training platforms that support RPDM. Also, since the number of emergent incidents is decreasing due to code improvements, the need to create virtual immersive emergent events is here to stay.

Research supports immersive training as beneficial for our environments. Immersive educational platforms can have numerous real-life scenarios that test and grade performance in an unbiased manner. Forward-facing organizational accountability, I think, will require meaningful consideration of developing a virtual reality training platform in most departments. Consideration of pilot programs is a minimum, and strategic plans for wholesale changes to how we conduct future training is perhaps one way we will increase reliability and resilience within our emergency response systems.

In Closing

I hope you have enjoyed and gained some benefit from reading this book. It has been my privilege and honor to assist with the development of fair and thorough review work in the fire service. I wish you all the good this life can offer. Please don't hesitate to reach out at MarkKeoughAZ@gmail.com.

If you want to learn how to facilitate reviews, please visit the Fire Department Safety Officers Association (FDSOA) website. FDSOA offers a 16-hour Conducting Reviews in The Fire Service course, with an option to do an additional 3 to 4-hour meeting with your department's leadership team. Contact FDSOA at *fdsoa.org* to arrange a class in your area.

Question Answers

Section One
1. B
2. D
3. F
4. F
5. T
6. F
7. B
8. A
9. C, D, B, A

Section Two
1. B, A, D
2. F
3. T
4. D
5. T
6. T
7. D
8. T
9. C
10. C
11. C
12. E
13. T
14. F
15. D
16. B
17. B
18. T

Section Three
1. F
2. A
3. C
4. D
5. D
6. C
7. T

Section Four
1. D
2. T
3. F
4. T

Section Five
1. T
2. C
3. B
4. B
5. D
6. E

Section Six
1. C
2. E
3. T
4. T
5. C

Section Seven
1. D
2. D
3. D
4. T
5. A
6. T
7. T
8. F
9. C
10. T
11. F
12. T